PRAISE FOR

Faith Is Not a Feeling

"The title of Ney's book says it all—Faith is not a feeling but a decision and a continuing discovery. There couldn't be a better time for this book to cross any believer's—or would-be believer's—path."

—PEGGY NOONAN, author of *When Character Was King*

"Profound in its simplicity, *Faith Is Not a Feeling* is a treasure-trove of practical gems for both young Christians and those who have long traveled the 'by faith' path."

—LINDA DILLOW, speaker and author of *Calm My Anxious Heart* and coauthor of *Intimate Issues*

"'Get Ney' is a phrase we often use when we need help in matters of faith. I know of no one whose life more exemplifies living by faith than Ney Bailey. This book introduces you to her, my remarkable, wonderful friend."

—LUCI SWINDOLL, author and speaker

"For over twenty-five years my dear friend Ney Bailey has provided words of comfort for my periodically frayed emotions. If you can't 'Get Ney,' get this book. You will be gently reminded that faith is rooted in God's unchangeable Word, not in our changeable feelings."

—MARILYN MEBERG, author and speaker

"We speak with our hearts and with our minds when we say that *Faith Is Not a Feeling* should be in every believer's library. It has had a profound impact on both of us!"

—JOSH and DOTTIE McDOWELL, authors

"One of the greatest joys of my life is calling Ney Bailey my friend. Ney's life and words are full of wisdom, grace, and compassion and come from a heart overflowing with love for Christ our Savior. This book is a solid apologetic for a faith based on rock, not sand. I highly commend it to you."

—SHEILA WALSH, speaker and author of *A Love So Big*

"A busy housewife with six young children, on being asked, 'Do you *feel* married?' replied, 'I don't know what I *feel,* but I know I *am!*' Ney takes us to the heart of the matter as she defines faith as taking God at His word, which can only come from a personal relationship with Him, quite independent of feelings—to the extent that in a crisis I can say, 'Thank You, God, for trusting me with this experience, even if You never tell me why.' As Ney says, this brings 'peace in the midst of turmoil.'"

—HELEN ROSEVEARE, author of *Give Me This Mountain* and *He Gave Us a Valley*

FAITH IS NOT
A FEELING

NEY BAILEY

CHOOSING TO TAKE GOD
AT HIS WORD

WaterBrook
PRESS

FAITH IS NOT A FEELING

All Scripture quotations, unless otherwise indicated, are taken from the *New American Standard Bible*® (NASB). © Copyright The Lockman Foundation 1960, 1962, 1963, 1968, 1971, 1972, 1973, 1975, 1977. Used by permission. (www.Lockman.org). Scripture quotations marked (TLB) are taken from *The Living Bible* copyright © 1971. Used by permission of Tyndale House Publishers, Inc., Wheaton, Illinois 60189. All rights reserved. Scripture quotations marked (NIV) are taken from the *Holy Bible, New International Version*®. NIV®. Copyright © 1973, 1978, 1984 by International Bible Society. Used by permission of Zondervan Publishing House. All rights reserved. Scripture quotations marked (KJV) are taken from the *King James Version*.

Trade Paperback ISBN 978-1-57856-343-2
eBook ISBN 978-0-307-56480-1

Copyright © 1978 Here's Life Publishers, Inc.
Copyright © 1993 Integrated Resources (revised edition)
Copyright © 2002 by Ney Bailey

Published in the United States by WaterBrook, an imprint of the Crown Publishing Group, a division of Penguin Random House LLC, New York.

WATERBROOK® and its deer colophon are registered trademarks of Penguin Random House LLC.

Library of Congress Catalog Card No. 78060077

Printed in the United States of America
1979—First edition, 11 printings
1993—Second edition, 4 printings
2003—Third edition, 1st printing

2017
20 19 18 17 16

It is with deep appreciation and a grateful heart
that I dedicate this book to my father and mother,

Ed and Alberta Bailey,

who have loved me and given themselves to me sacrificially.

———————————

CONTENTS

CONTENTS

FOREWORD

Ney Bailey is one of God's special ambassadors. I first met Ney in 1961 when she left her native Louisiana and her profession as an adoption caseworker to join the staff of Campus Crusade for Christ. In the ensuing forty years she has served on our campus staff at the University of Arizona, initiated and directed our Human Resources department, and helped to pioneer a pre-marriage and family emphasis within our ministry. Since 1969 she has traveled as a representative throughout the United States and has gone all over the world bearing the message of Jesus Christ and encouraging thousands to follow Him. Ney has made a vital contribution to this ministry and to our staff with her habitual attitude of "What can I do to help make things better?"

Everywhere Ney goes she gives two things: her heart and her knowledge of God's Word. The biblical principles she shares are grounded in personal experience, and there is ample proof that they have changed many lives.

I often hear the positive results of Ney's ministry, and I often seek her counsel. Thus, I was personally delighted when I learned that she was writing a book. *Faith Is Not a Feeling* provides solid scriptural teaching on a life of faith. Having experienced the impact that walking by faith has had in my own life and ministry, I see an urgent need for a book with this message.

Our feelings and God's Word do not always coincide. Ney gives insight into why this is so and how the conflict can be resolved. She gives practical help and input no matter where a person is on his or her pilgrimage with the Lord.

This is a very personal, interesting, and fast-moving book. It combines tragedy, humor, and drama in a way that holds the reader's interest. First published in 1979, *Faith Is Not a Feeling* has consistently been in print and is now a classic. I predict that you will want to read and reread this book and recommend it to others. I highly commend it to you.

Bill Bright
Founder/Chairman
Campus Crusade for Christ International

ACKNOWLEDGMENTS

It is with the deepest appreciation and heartfelt gratitude that I acknowledge:

My family—especially my parents and Brenda, Ed, and Kim—for reading and giving suggestions on portions of the manuscript.

Mary Graham—my dear friend with whom I share a home. During my writing and rewriting she has demonstrated great love and patience. I have appreciated her honesty and constructive suggestions. She should receive special recognition for being a discerning sounding board who has counseled me wisely and given valuable editorial assistance.

Liz Heaney—my editor for this WaterBrook revised edition. She has been above and beyond all I could ask or think. I have marveled at her giftedness and her expertise and have been honored to work with her. All who know her say she is one of the best there is. And she is.

Linda Dillow—my dear, wonderful friend who, in the midst of her own very busy writing and speaking schedule, graciously offered to write the twelve-week Bible study in the back of the book. Linda is an outstanding Bible teacher and has given all of us a good gift.

Dan Rich—for having a vision for the revised, updated version of this book.

Lisa Guest and Carol Bartley—for their kindness and perfectionism in the copyediting process.

The WaterBrook team—for their professionalism and hard work in moving the book through the process to publication and distribution.

Judy Downs Douglass—my longtime friend who encouraged me to write down what I had been speaking about.

Janet Kobobel Grant—who did the final editing on the original edition.

Frank Allnut—for his confidence in me and for overseeing the original publication of this book.

Sharon Fischer—my editor on the first edition of this book. She gave me excellent advice and suggestions and had a way of asking the right questions to draw out more detail and make my material more readable. She gave of her time and herself. She became more to me than my editor—she became my friend.

Bill and Vonette Bright—for allowing me to join the staff of Campus Crusade in the early years when there were only 100 of us, for being an example to all of us to believe God for great things, and for providing spiritual food and an atmosphere of love and acceptance so that I could begin to grow up in Christ while on staff. I will be devoted to both of them as long as I live.

Tina Hood—my marvelous assistant and friend. She had the heart to come alongside and help me in my ministry and on this project. I'm very grateful for her and all the hours she has invested in His Kingdom on my behalf.

Winky Leinster—my dear friend of many years who invested countless hours with me proofreading and helping with the first revision of the original manuscript. Her meticulous attention to detail was a great asset.

Jean Pietsch Prensner—my faithful friend and partner in ministry. She helped me recall some of the incidents we shared in our years together. God continues to bless me with her encouragement, wise counsel, and prayers. Our lives are forever intertwined.

David A. Sunde—my colleague and dear friend who agreed to read the manuscript "slowly, carefully, and purposefully" for theological accuracy. I am grateful for his encouragement and for his investment of time on my behalf.

Sallie Clingman—my longtime friend who has taught me many things about the Lord and who was the one God used to name this book.

Don and Sally Meredith—for their valuable input into my life in the area of relationships and for their utterly faithful friendship in spite of great distances and long absences.

Hav and Dotty Larson—for the privilege of living in their summer home at Lake Arrowhead, California, for eight years, including the months when I wrote this book. The quiet, restful retreat atmosphere, the view of the lake, the birds, squirrels, and tall pine trees made it the perfect place to write. The Larsons are among those I hold dear.

Carol Rhoad—our dear friend who was the first to help me type the material for the book. The last day we spent together is where this book begins...

INTRODUCTION

"What would you do if you only had a year to live?" Paul Eshleman asked a group of us in a staff meeting.

I thought, *I would try to put into print some of the things I have been speaking on because they seem to be ministering so powerfully in people's lives.* Soon after that, Judy Downs Douglass, then with Campus Crusade's publications department and now wife of the president of Campus Crusade, told me, "Ney, we are interested in your writing a book based on the content of your messages."

Then Sharon Fischer, also in our publications department, commented to a mutual friend, "I've heard some of Ney's tapes. The things she is speaking on cross the lines of male, female, single, married. They apply to all of us. If she ever writes a book, I'd really like to work with her on it."

And so the Lord began to put this book together.

In the nearly twenty-five years since this book was first published, I have marveled as God has sent these words out around the world. I have been delighted to see that He does indeed fashion our hearts alike and that the biblical principles within these pages are timeless and universal in application.

Feelings are a part of each of us. They can be either friend or foe, depending on how we utilize them. Come with me now as I share with you some of the struggles and trials I've had in learning how to harness and channel my feelings. Come with me as I share how I've learned to use them as an avenue to take me to God's Word.

Thousands of people who have heard the words on the following pages have come to me, called me, or written me to say that their lives will never be the same after hearing these truths. As you read this book, I pray that you will be encouraged and challenged, that God will strike fire in your heart, and that your life will be changed because you can say, "Now I understand what it means to walk by faith. I understand that faith is not a feeling but a choice to take God at His word."

Ney Bailey

CHAPTER 1

THE FLOOD

"Evacuate immediately! Evacuate immediately!" Those terrifying words from the night before resounded in my head as I listened intently to the television newscast:

July 31, 1976. The Big Thompson runs wild, over its banks. One hundred people are dead, 800 missing. Property damage is in the millions—the worst disaster in Colorado state history. A freak rainstorm on the eastern face of the Continental Divide dumps fourteen inches of rain in six hours from Estes Park to Loveland, just north of Denver. A wall of water hurtles down the canyon, pushed by a wailing, moaning wind. Trees are uprooted, homes and autos smashed to pieces. Rescue efforts bog down. Rescuers go airborne, searching desperately for the missing. The air itself is a mixture of sewage, diesel fuel, and human cries.

By August first it was all over but the search.... The flood that experts thought impossible had hit. Surging waters had turned a pastoral scene into a nightmare landscape. There would be prayers of thanksgiving for the survivors, prayers of grief for those not as fortunate.

As I watched the news report from the safety of my apartment in Fort Collins, Colorado, images from the night before filled my mind. How close I'd come to being a victim of that flood! Just hours earlier I had been running from its waters, desperate to reach higher ground. As I sat safely in my cozy apartment, I could hardly believe that I'd come so close to death. Once again I thanked God for being with me and for guiding my friends and me to safety.

Over the next several days, however, I learned that seven of the dearest people I knew had died in that flood.

Just the day before, thirty-five women in leadership positions with Campus Crusade for Christ had been relaxing and enjoying an overnight retreat at the Sylvan Dale Ranch in the Big Thompson Canyon near Loveland, Colorado. We had eagerly anticipated this reunion as a time to catch up with each other before our annual staff training at Colorado State University in Fort Collins. Staff members had come from all over the United States. Many had just returned from overseas assignments.

We arrived at the ranch around noon on July 31, welcomed by a sign at its entrance that read, "Spend cool restful nights away from highway noise." The weather was perfect. A bristling pine scent filled the mountain air. A warm sun eased its way through the Rocky Mountains' clear blue skies onto our ranch, which was nestled in a valley at about five thousand feet elevation. Through the Narrows, a sheer rock canyon towering next to the ranch, rushed the Big Thompson River.

After a relaxing lunch in the dining room overlooking the river, we went horseback riding and swimming. Then we climbed aboard a pile of hay on a wagon and sang and laughed and talked as we wound up a narrow canyon road along the river to a waterfall and then back down to the ranch for the evening meal.

During dinner I gazed out a window, intrigued by a silver-haired woman fly-fishing in the river. She was standing on some rocks in the riverbed, her pants legs rolled up and her friends encouraging her on. *How,* I wondered, *could she hope to catch any fish in such fast-running water that was so shallow?*

After a home-cooked barbecue chicken dinner, our group gathered near a large stone fireplace in the spacious meeting room of the People's Barn, a quaint structure facing the riverbank and decorated on the outside with large old wagon wheels. As we talked and shared stories together, none of us had any idea that the next few hours and days would change our lives. Joy filled the room as we reflected on all God had done for us through the year.

When it was Carol Rhoad's time to talk, she told us about her afternoon. Tired and needing rest, she had taken a nap and had missed the hayride. When she woke up, she went on a walk around the ranch and met one of the ranch owners, who said to her, "We have people here all the time, but I have never seen a group so happy, so peaceful, so beautiful. Who are you?" Carol had an opportunity to tell him that Jesus was the Source of our joy, and then she went on to explain how he could know Jesus Christ personally. At the time none of us realized that in just a matter of hours Carol would be with Jesus Christ—forever.

When Carol finished, Marilyn Henderson[1] described her hopes and dreams for the upcoming staff training. She told us she had prayed that all of us would be changed that weekend.

About 9:15 P.M. we took a leisurely coffee break. A few minutes after we had reassembled, I heard a siren ringing faintly in the distance. Within moments the siren grew louder, and I heard something being announced over a megaphone. As the noisy chorus approached, I began to distinguish the words: "THIS IS THE POLICE. EVACUATE IMMEDIATELY! THE RIVER IS RISING! A FLOOD IS COMING THIS WAY!"

The day had been tranquil and sunny, except for some clouds and a light sprinkling about dinnertime. How could we be in danger of a flood? *It's a joke,* I thought.

Then someone said, "I went outside at the coffee break, and the river did look a little funny…"

Outside, the police continued to bellow orders in desperate repetition: "EVACUATE IMMEDIATELY! HIGH WATER IS COMING! DON'T TAKE ANYTHING WITH YOU! GET TO HIGHER GROUND!"

As we realized that the flood warning was no joke, the room became electric with action. In less than a minute, we abandoned the People's Barn and dashed into the darkness. Intending to drive to higher ground, all of us piled into our eight cars parked just outside the door. None of us knew the area, so we had no idea where to go. We had no time to talk or make a plan. We later learned that in the confusion we all had heard different instructions.

I saw a police car headed for a bridge and decided to follow him. My car and three others crossed the bridge and went up to a store parking lot by Highway 34. When we reached the parking lot, my car lights illuminated a policeman in a yellow rain slicker, urgently shouting orders into a megaphone: "GET TO HIGHER GROUND! FLOODWATERS ARE COMING!" One of my passengers was going to hop out to ask which direction we should head when we heard someone standing nearby cry out, "The bridge we just crossed—it's gone!" Water now covered the area we had just left.

Above the din of car engines running, people shouting, and propane tanks exploding as they bobbed down the river, I yelled out the window, "Where is higher ground?"

The policeman didn't answer me but just continued his frantic announcement: "CAN'T YOU HEAR THOSE TANKS EXPLODING? GET OUT OF HERE! GET OUT OF YOUR CARS, AND GET TO HIGHER GROUND!"

I got out of my car and called to him again, "Where is higher ground? Can anyone help us?" Again, no answer.

I knew the ground rose somewhere on the other side of the road near the parking lot because I had seen it earlier in the day. But where was that higher ground?

The air smelled of propane gas. We were in danger from the propane tanks that had been torn off of house trailers and homes and were floating down the river. They were exploding as they hit barriers. I could taste the gas in my mouth.

We got out of our car and in the darkness and rain and confusion managed to grope our way up a steep hill in straggling formation. We struggled to get to the top, fighting barbed wire and slipping and sliding in the mud. Lightning flashes intermittently relieved the stormy blackness, making it difficult for our eyes to adjust to the darkness.

Afraid of getting separated in the chaos, I held Winky Leinster's hand and guided her up the steep slope. We glanced back to see Jackie Hudson bending down to aid an elderly woman who was helplessly battling the wet mud, struggling to maneuver through a treacherous wire fence.

I felt as if the raging water was following us, nipping at our heels, threatening to swallow us any minute as we struggled to escape. I had never come so close to death.

Finally eight of us reached the top and huddled together, relieved that we had made it to higher ground but concerned about the rest of the women in our group. What had happened to the other two cars that had left the ranch with us? And what had happened to the rest of our group? Were they safe? Were *we* safe? Would the floodwaters rise this high? Biting winds and pelting rain intensified the chill of the cold mountain air. I had always hated to be cold, but I tried not to think about it. We sat clustered on a boulder, trying to shelter each other from the pounding elements.

I knew there was only one thing we could do, so I said, "Let's pray." With a sense of the authority of Scripture undergirding me, I began, "Lord, Your Word says, in everything give thanks, because this is the will of God in Christ Jesus concerning us.[2] So while we are in this, we choose with our wills to thank You.

"And, Lord, Your Word says that all things—including this—work together for good to those who love You—and we do—and are called according to Your purpose[3]—and we are. You have also said that heaven and earth will pass away but Your Word will not pass away.[4] So Your Word is truer than anything we are feeling or experiencing right now."

As we prayed, a peace settled over us as God calmed our fears and comforted our hearts. We began to sing the praise chorus "Father, I Adore You." In the depths of our hearts we laid our lives before Him.

We then went back down the hill a short way to join a group of tourists who had found better shelter near some high rocks.

From there we watched the eerie flashing of headlights from campers and cars being carried down the river and propane tanks detonating in sudden, fiery bursts of light.

I noticed that one of the tourists was the older woman Jackie had helped through the fence. I gave her a big hug and exclaimed, "I'm so glad you're okay!"

"Who are you, and why are you being so good to me?" she asked.

Without hesitation I said, "I would hope that if my mother were ever caught in something like this, someone would be there to help—"

Just then the police signaled for us to come back down to the road below. They told us the floodwaters had receded and we could return to our cars. Though the raging river had overflowed its banks, the water had not reached our vehicles. We got back in our cars, and once again I followed a patrol car as we headed back to Loveland on a narrow road away from the river.

But as we approached Loveland, we saw the flashing red lights of a police barricade, and an officer flagged us on to Fort Collins. They were not letting cars stop in Loveland.

We arrived in Fort Collins after midnight and immediately checked with the sheriff's office to ask about the safety of the others who had been at our retreat. An officer assured us that the Sylvan Dale Ranch had been evacuated safely. While the others went back to the Colorado State campus, Jackie and I headed back to the ranch to look for our friends and to see if there was anything we could do to help. We were on our way when we heard on the radio that everyone was being advised to stay away from the area. About the same time a police barricade stopped us, and the officers told us to turn back. That settled it. Realizing there was nothing else we could do, we turned back and went home to our apartments near the campus.

As soon as I got home, I tried to call Marilyn, who lived in the apartment across the hall from me. Marilyn had been my roommate and was a close friend and colleague. I wanted to be sure that she and the others were okay. She didn't answer, and I grew anxious. Where was she? Why wasn't she home? Was she safe? I decided to put a note on her door, telling her to awaken me when she came back, and then I went to bed, exhausted. It was 3 A.M.

I woke up six hours later when Winky Leinster knocked on my door. When I let her in, she told me the shocking news: Some of the women at our retreat were believed missing. I dressed as quickly as possible, called my family to assure them of my safety, and Winky and I raced to the office of the president of Campus Crusade.

As I came up to Dr. Bill Bright's door, staff members hugged me, telling me they were grateful just to see me alive. I burst into tears. It had been twelve hours since the warning sirens rang out along the riverbank, but I was still in shock.

Dr. Bright welcomed me into his office. The atmosphere was solemn but peaceful. "Ney, I'm so glad to see that you're safe. How did you get out?" he asked.

"I followed a police car out on a back road." I explained that in the confusion only four of our cars had followed the police out of the retreat center.

"Marilyn called about midnight to tell us she was in the hospital," he said soberly. "Later they brought in Melanie."

The news stunned me, leaving me bewildered. "What do you mean, they're in the hospital?"

"Their car went into the water. Both Marilyn and Melanie were able to hang on to trees until someone rescued them, but they aren't sure that anyone else made it."

"Their car went into the water?" I couldn't keep the shock from my voice. Marilyn's car had been in the group that drove off the ranch. How had it gone into the floodwaters?

"Marilyn told us that the police had said to go east, toward Loveland."

"East toward Loveland!" I exclaimed. I sat motionless, my mouth open in disbelief. They had headed directly into the path of the floodwaters!

Then he told me, "We still haven't heard about the other cars or their passengers." The moment was profoundly sober because Dr. Bright's wife, Vonette, was one of the missing.

Just then the phone rang. Dr. Bright listened solemnly, then placed his hand over the mouthpiece and reported, "They've positively identified the bodies of Carol Rhoad and Cathie Loomis."

I slumped back in the chair as if I had been hit with a thousand-pound weight. How could this have happened? The unreality of the night before was spilling over into this Sunday morning.

I talked with Dr. Bright a few more minutes, then hurried to the hospital to see Marilyn.

When I entered her room, she smiled weakly. She was bruised and exhausted, spitting up mud and debris from the violent river that had tried to claim her life. I sat with Marilyn for several hours, and she told me what she'd been through the night before. A policeman had stuck his head in her car window and told her to head toward Loveland. She did, and as they were following another car across a bridge, a huge wall of water had come over the bridge and swept them into the turbulent Big Thompson River.

What she told me next amazed me. "All of us saw the water coming before it swept our car off the bridge, and as it tumbled toward us, we were praying, 'Lord, we thank You that we belong to You. We know that You love us even though this is happening to us.'"

Peace in the midst of turmoil.

Marilyn went on to tell me that she and Melanie managed to open their windows and escape from the car. She pulled Carol out, but then the water carried her away before she was able to reach Precy or June in the backseat. She was swept about a quarter mile downstream before she was able to cling to a tree. Just when she felt as if she couldn't hold on any longer, lights shone on her, and she was rescued. She told the rescuers about the other women in the car, but the only one they had found was Melanie.

Before leaving the hospital to pick up Mary Graham, another close friend and coworker, at the Denver Stapleton Airport, I prayed for Marilyn and for our dear friends who were still missing.

As I drove, dark clouds gathered, and rain started pouring down. It was as if God was mourning too.

Mary hadn't been at our retreat because of a prior commitment, and she had arranged for either Carol or me to meet her plane. I wanted Mary to hear from me why Carol wasn't there.

I had been in airports all over the country, hundreds of times, but this time was different. Just the day before I had basked in the Colorado sun with some dear friends, and we had praised God for His goodness and His creation. Now here I was, a survivor of a devastating flood that had taken the lives of at least two of our friends—and maybe more.

As I walked to the gate, my heart was breaking. I couldn't help but wonder how many times I had passed people in airports who had just lost someone dear to them, and I hadn't known what they were going through.

When Mary walked off the plane, I burst into tears again. She had heard about the flood in Big Thompson Canyon from a fellow passenger, but she'd had no idea that the floodwaters had reached Sylvan Dale Ranch. She was shocked and disbelieving. How could this have happened? And how could it have happened to us? In stunned silence we claimed her bags from the carousel.

Over the next few days, we began to piece together what had happened that night. Only minutes after we evacuated it, mud and water filled the People's Barn. Although another driver and I had been told to get out of our cars and head to higher ground, the two other cars that had left the ranch with us were told to "go east toward Loveland." The four other cars, carrying seventeen of our women, drove to higher ground on the ranch. When the floodwaters subsided, they managed to find each other in the darkness and spent the night in the retreat center's recreation hall. All of them, including Vonette Bright, hiked out to safety the next afternoon.

But the cars that headed for Loveland met disaster. As they were crossing a bridge, a wall of water crashed over the road, sweeping both cars into the river. Both cars sank within seconds. Seven of the nine women in those cars lost their lives. Only Marilyn and Melanie survived.

I had read somewhere that whatever brings us the greatest joy also brings us the greatest sorrow. I knew this to be true as I cried over the death of my friends. I sobbed. I was brokenhearted. I had loved them dearly.

Vivid memories of each one came back.

Rae Ann Johnston... During a meeting that morning, I had slipped her a note asking her to room with me at the retreat. The note was tucked away in my Bible with her response: "I'd love to."

Carol Rhoad... She had joyfully served as the administrative assistant for the women on the U.S. National Campus Team. She brought a touch of home to our meetings—surprises of fruit, cheese, flowers. Earlier in the summer I had given a four-week series of talks, and Carol had invited some friends. They had all sat in the front row each time, cheering me on.

Cathie Loomis... She was sitting by me in the People's Barn during the coffee break. I remember thinking, *I have never seen Cathie so radiantly beautiful.*

June Fujiwara... Her eyes disappeared when she smiled her lovely Hawaiian smile. She stayed at my home in California one December. I snapped a picture of her on snow skis for the first time in her life.

Precy Manongdo... Our Campus Crusade representative in the Philippines. The day of the flood she and I had leaned over a fence, chatting and watching a stream go by, as we waited for our horses to be saddled.

Barbie Leyden... She had delighted me ever since I met her. Barbie had created a fictitious character named Edith. If the dishes didn't get done, she blamed Edith's negligence. If the car keys were missing, Edith had taken them. One summer we planned a birthday party for Edith, promising all the invited guests that she would actually appear. After refreshments we arranged for a telegram to be delivered—from Edith. The closing line read, "You can't have your cake and Edith too."

Terri Bissing… During a difficult two-week period in my life, she sent me a card and special note every day in the mail. At the retreat we had planned to have a good visit.

Each one, a dear friend. Each one, now gone.

In the weeks that followed, I knew I could become bitter and cynical if I demanded to know why this tragedy had happened. I also knew that we become bitter to the degree that we don't give thanks. So, through tears, I began to offer a sacrifice of thanksgiving[5] to God. I purposed to focus on what He had given rather than on what I had lost.

I could have lived my life without ever knowing and loving these dear women, yet God had allowed me to enjoy them. He had given me the gift of time spent with each person. I could thank Him for that.

Over and over again I had to choose with my will—not my feelings—to give thanks. God, in His Word, had promised that He would work all things—including this tragedy—together for good to those who love Him and are called according to His purpose.

A month or so after the flood, a friend wrote, "Ney, if I had been in that flood, I don't know if I could have responded as you did." I was deeply aware that God had supernaturally given me the courage and strength to go on, to look for the good and to praise Him for His goodness in spite of the circumstances. I held firmly to this truth: *God's Word is truer than how I feel.* I was deeply aware that my response was the result of many lessons I had learned the hard way—by my mistakes.

CHAPTER 2

ARIZONA
AGONY

My navy blue Volkswagen was packed to the gills. I had stuffed most of my earthly belongings into my little car and a four-by-eight trailer and was driving seventeen hundred miles from my home in New Orleans, across West Texas and New Mexico, into Arizona and Tucson.

I was twenty-five years old—young, confident, and full of hope. I had become a Christian when I was fifteen, but I hadn't been serious about my faith until a year and a half before. I had graduated from college and was working in New Orleans as an adoption caseworker when a friend of mine began to talk with me about her relationship with God, and I realized that her relationship with Him sounded so much more personal and meaningful than mine. I wanted to know more about how to have that kind of relationship. In time, I came to understand that knowing God was more than knowing *about* Him. As a result of my friend's influence, I started reading the Bible and going to church, and my relationship with God became real and life-changing.

As I grew in my understanding of God's love for me and His forgiveness, a strong desire to tell others about Him grew as well. I longed for others to know all they could have in Christ. So I resigned my job at the adoption agency and joined the staff of Campus Crusade. Now I was about to begin my first assignment as a staff member on the University of Arizona campus. During those lonely hours on the road, my excitement grew as I thought about the year ahead.

I drove to Arizona with a dream in my heart. As I understood it, I was responsible for meeting with college students, particularly students in leadership positions, and being a spiritual resource to them. I thought, *First I'll talk to all the sorority presidents, all the women who are in student government, and the presidents of all the student organizations.* That seemed easy. I'd held similar positions as a student, and if someone had come to me then, I would have been grateful to hear that God loves me and wants to remove my guilt and shame. This had been great news to me, and I was zealous to tell everyone everywhere. I just knew it would be great news to them!

I'd always been the kind of person who rose to a challenge, and I had no doubt that working with university students would be a big one, but I was eager to face it. After all, I found it easy to meet new people, build relationships, and engage others in meaningful conversations. I took it for granted that I would walk onto the U of A campus, meet every female student, become her friend, and talk to her about God's love—and they would all respond exactly as I had.

But it didn't turn out to be so easy. I was young, naive, and wrong—dead wrong.

At our staff conference the month before, one of the conference leaders had interviewed me and asked, "What do you think is your greatest need as you look forward to your assignment?"

Without hesitating, I replied, "To be trained in how to have a campus ministry. Since I've never seen one, I have a lot to learn." I'd been impressed with the caliber of men and women I'd met at the conference. I felt inspired by their lives and ministries. They were articulate about their faith. They could answer hard questions about knowing God. They were skilled at helping others grow spiritually. In matters of personal faith, they seemed like experts to me, and I wanted to be like them. I also wanted to help others be like that.

I was sincere and full of energy. I just knew that God had great things in store for me this year. I anticipated success in this new venture. I had no reason to expect anything else. Yet, as I crossed the desert, I was driving toward the biggest shock and disappointment of my life.

I'd heard a lot about Arizona's year-round sun and exquisite sunsets. As I drove, I saw hundreds of large saguaro cacti decorating valleys framed by hills and mountains in the distance. I loved the state already.

A thoughtful couple in Tucson had rented a one-room apartment for me, adjacent to one of the university's largest dormitories. All I knew about the U of A was that the previous year it had been voted the number-one party school in the nation by *Playboy* magazine. But as I entered Tucson and drove past the university toward my apartment, I saw lovely, old brick buildings and tall palm trees interspersed with large cypress trees. The campus was beautiful.

I arrived eager to jump into my training and learn everything there was to know, which I figured was a lot! Paul Schipper, a fellow staff member, had been assigned to work on campus with me. I looked forward to the training and insight I would gain from working with him and the student who had initiated the campus ministry. But within days of our arrival, the tables were turned. Our student leader decided to devote his full attention to graduate studies, and he turned the entire university ministry over to Paul and me. Then Paul was sent 120 miles north to Arizona State University to be trained by the area's staff director.

That left me at the University of Arizona in unfamiliar Tucson—ALONE. Even though I'd just arrived, I alone was responsible for running the entire campus ministry. This was not what I'd had in mind! I was a young Christian and ignorant about how to lead a campus ministry. Campus Crusade was also young; at that time we had minimal training and only a small staff. There was no one to help me. I was on my own to reach students for Christ and to help them figure out how to reach their friends and fellow students. Uh-oh!

I wanted to do well, and I knew Campus Crusade expected me to succeed. After all, they had trusted me to be alone on this huge campus. I was supposed to be spending my days with students, one-on-one. Theoretically, I'd meet young women, have a soft drink with them, and build a relationship that would enable me to help them become stronger in their faith. We would study the Bible together, they would get excited about how much God loved them, and then I'd help them know how they could reach others. They'd have disciples of their own, and the cycle would continue until eventually everyone at the U of A would have heard the gospel from a fellow student. Then, I guess, we'd all be off to tell the world. I had such a passion that at the time it seemed fairly simple.

Until I learned it wasn't.

I had to telephone students in order to make appointments with them, but I hated calling people I didn't know and asking them to meet me. It seemed forced and artificial. I was used to sharing Christ with people I already knew. I felt increasingly uncomfortable with this new approach. Every night I would stare at the black phone in my apartment as if it were a five-hundred-pound monster. I would sit by it for a long time, looking at names I could call. I knew I should be calling and making appointments, but something in me just couldn't do it.

If anyone in Campus Crusade had known how I was feeling and what was happening, I'm sure they could have helped. But I couldn't bring myself to tell anyone. I knew they thought I was capable, and I didn't want to disappoint them. So I grew even more fearful and tense.

The pressure only intensified when I compared myself to others on staff, particularly Diane. I saw her as the ideal staff member—highly successful in her ministry and always on top of things. She seemed undaunted about approaching people she didn't know and telling them about Christ. She spoke in sororities, discipled student leaders, and always knew exactly what to do on any campus. A lovely person in every way, she knew the Word of God and seemed to talk with others about Christ freely and easily. In my mind, Diane was at the top of the scale of effectiveness, and I landed at the bottom.

But worse than my fears or feelings of inadequacy was my disillusionment with God. I felt that He had let me down. Hadn't I left everything to follow Him? My family, my friends, my security? Why was my life falling apart? I felt discouraged, unhappy, and defeated. Is this what it meant to serve Him?

As a student and as an adoption caseworker, I seemed to have an intuitive sense about how to succeed, and I had assumed that I'd be as comfortable discipling students. In addition to my natural abilities, I'd have something else going for me! I thought God Himself would help me be more successful than I'd ever been before.

But here I was, ready to quit after only a month at the university. How had this happened to me? I'd never failed before—at least not that I'd been willing to admit.

In high school I had failed algebra, but "only because the teacher was so hard." I enrolled again with another teacher and passed the course, proving my point.

I did have a little taste of failure in college, but I had managed to survive. I had auditioned for the choir, a prestigious group held in high regard all over the state of Louisiana. The director ran me through some scales and then assigned me to the alto section, possibly because I could hit some low notes and he needed altos. Since I couldn't read music very well, I stayed close to the other altos and depended on them for pitch and cues during preseason practice at choir camp.

I was able to sing the alto part just fine until the director rearranged everyone and placed me between a soprano and a tenor. I was so used to listening to the people around me to help me sing my part that I kept singing the tenor and soprano parts instead of the alto. Alarmed that someone would notice and decide I shouldn't be in the choir, I started to lip sync during our rehearsals. I never sang unless I was absolutely sure of my note.

Real panic set in when the director announced the choir's performing plans for the year. Besides the normal round of traveling concerts, we were scheduled to sing on a weekly television program and would possibly be selected by the government for a tour of Asian military bases.

That was when I made my decision: I couldn't stay in the choir and fake it, not with that kind of itinerary. I had to do something, but I couldn't just admit the truth. After mulling over every possible face-saving retreat from the choir, a solution came to me—one that would guarantee my dismissal.

The next time I was alone at the sorority house, I placed a three-foot stool in the middle of the living room and began jumping off the stool, over and over. I desperately wanted to break my ankle so I would be excused from the performances. Years before I'd hurt my ankle on a hiking trip, and I thought it would be easy to reinjure it.

My plan worked! I sprained my ankle and was released from the choir.

Now I was in a similar predicament: I was out of my league and too embarrassed to say so. I didn't want to admit failure. What would people think? How could I write Bill Bright and tell him I hated being in Arizona and wanted to leave? Friends back home were praying for me and investing financially in my ministry. How could I possibly write them and say I wasn't going through with my assignment? I was overwhelmed. Not even a sprained ankle was going to get me out of this one!

Late one afternoon I was lying down on the rug in my apartment, my chin resting on my crossed arms. I could see lines on the wall marking where my bed opened out of the wall. My eyes spotted the gas heater on the next wall. I thought, *I'll just turn on that gas heater, and it will all be over. All my misery will be gone…*

No, that would never do, because what if the Tucson newspaper headlines read, "Campus Crusade Staff Member Commits Suicide"? That could reflect negatively on Campus Crusade, on Christ, on me.

My thoughts drifted to the mountain range near Tucson. *I'll go up to Mt. Lemon in my little Volkswagen and just happen to be driving down the mountain, and I'll go off the side… It'll look like an accident! And everyone will say, "Poor Ney. She was out for a leisurely drive on the mountain and somehow lost control of the car."* There! No negative reflection on me, on Campus Crusade, or on God.

While I obviously didn't commit suicide, my deep depression lingered. I was convinced that the problem was the campus and the fact that I was alone. I prayed, "Lord, if I can ever get out of this place, I'll never come back."

The first of November came, and I was assigned to Arizona State University for training. *If only I can get up there,* I told myself, *everything will be all right.* But the change in location didn't solve my problems. If you take a rotten apple and fly it from Tucson to Phoenix, it's still rotten when it gets there. I hated being at Arizona State too. I was still depressed, still afraid, and still feeling like a failure. Slowly I began to realize that whatever was wrong was *inside me.*

One day, when I was scheduled to be on the ASU campus, I defiantly jumped into my Volkswagen, drove to Phoenix, found a coffee shop, and ordered the biggest hot fudge sundae on the menu.

"Here I am, eating this hot fudge sundae," I proclaimed with belligerence. "Nobody knows I'm here, I don't need these calories, and I DON'T CARE!"

I had been invited to be in the wedding of a childhood friend,

Bev, in Corpus Christi, Texas, at Christmastime. I mentioned the wedding to the state director, Elmer Lappen, when we met for our weekly appointment in the library.

"When I go home for Christmas to be in Bill and Bev's wedding, I think I'll stay there and not come back."

Elmer looked at me sadly. "Ney, if you do that, it will break my heart." And I thought firmly, *I care more about getting out of here than I do about breaking anyone's heart.* As I sat there needing help, I was silent. I was so afraid to admit my fears and sense of failure. All I wanted to do was run away.

At long last December 15 arrived, the day of my departure for the wedding and Christmas vacation. I had never been so glad to leave a place. I jumped in my VW, hit the city limits of Tucson, stopped, bought a package of Kents and a package of Salems, and smoked all the way to Corpus Christi! By the time I arrived at the wedding rehearsal, I smelled like a tobacco factory. The bizarre truth is, I'd rarely ever smoked before except for a few cigarettes in graduate school. I was desperate.

At the rehearsal dinner, someone suggested that we each mention briefly what Bev meant to us. I loved her dearly, but that night I was tongue-tied. More than anyone, Bev had influenced me to join the Campus Crusade staff. I was miserable and reasoned that she had contributed to my state of mind. I couldn't say a word that night and left there feeling even worse!

After the wedding, I headed for my parents' home in Shreveport, Louisiana. I barely enjoyed Christmas and moped around the house for two weeks. One day, as the end of my vacation approached, I found myself sitting on our living room couch, gazing toward the dining room and occasionally out the living room's picture window, feeling sorry for myself and dreading the thought of returning to Arizona.

I held up my hand and began to count on my fingers. "September, October, November, December... Let's see, I've made it through four months." I continued counting. "January, February, March, April, May... If I've made it through four months, I guess I can make it through five more. But in May, I'm gone."

Driving back to Arizona was one of the hardest things I've ever done. I felt like a total failure, but at least I wouldn't quit midstream. Awaiting me at my apartment was a letter from a friend in the navy who was stationed in Hawaii. He wrote, "Ney, I recently heard a man speak who helped me tremendously. His name is Merv Rosell, and for me, he was God's man with God's message at just the right time. He's going to be in Phoenix, and I want you to hear him."

I thought, *If there's ever anything I've needed, it's God's man with God's message—and this has got to be the right time.*

Within a week I was on my way to hear this man. I remember thinking in the car, *Lord, even though I am a missionary, if I need to, I'll walk down an aisle tonight to get right with You. I'm willing to do whatever You want me to do.*

I arrived at the meeting, not believing my ears as I heard the subject of his evening message: "Defeated Christians."

Rosell began, "If you have ever felt defeated in your Christian walk, this message is for you." I listened as if I were the only person in the room. He spoke of trying to live the Christian life on one's own resources, through self-effort. And he remarked that God often allows failure to point us to one crucial truth: that we cannot live the Christian life on our own power.

In conclusion, he said, "If you want to live for Jesus Christ this year, and the rest of your life, and if you want Jesus Christ to begin to live through you, I want you to stand."

I had been in other meetings where people were invited to respond. Usually I looked around self-consciously just to see what others did.

But this night I didn't care. It dawned on me that I had been trying to live the Christian life all by myself, depending on my own efforts. I realized I had gone to Arizona full of self-confidence. I'd had a picture in my mind of what it would be like. My expectations had been well-defined and my hopes high. When life turned out to be quite the opposite, I was stunned. In my utter disappointment, I berated myself and tried to hide from God and others. I needed to humble myself and ask for help instead of trying to struggle along on my own.

This speaker was telling me I could trust in Christ, not in myself and my own efforts. I wasn't exactly sure what that meant, but I was willing to try anything. When he said Christ could live His life through me, I desperately wanted that. I rose to my feet and in that moment asked the Lord Jesus Christ to take control of my life.

As I look back, I think this was the beginning of my understanding of what we sometimes refer to as the ministry of the Holy Spirit. When Christ comes into our lives, He obviously doesn't come in bodily; He comes into our lives by His Spirit. Once we have trusted Christ as our Savior and received His Spirit, we can either continue to run our own lives, depending on ourselves, or we can ask Him to run our lives—to be the director, the engineer, the controlling factor, the power source.

During my long months of agony, I had forgotten to trust God's Word. Jesus had promised He would always be with me, yet I had felt as if I had been all alone through those first months in Tucson. But He who said, "I will never desert you, nor will I ever forsake you"[1] and "I am with you always"[2] had been with me all along—even when I didn't recognize His presence. I was encouraged and comforted by the words of Jacob, who after a time of struggle said, "Surely the LORD is in this place, and I did not know it."[3]

God wasn't surprised that I had been in the wilderness. He had led me there. Though I had gone to Arizona with pure intentions, following the Lord as best I knew how, I had gone in my own power, on the strength of my own merits, and with my own desires and expectations. And God had allowed me to fail miserably, so much that I had wanted to die. He had let me hit the depths.

But out of those depths of frustration, I called upon Him. And He answered, revealing to me that there was only one person who had lived perfectly the Christian life—Jesus Christ Himself. When I began asking Christ to live His life through me, by the power of His Spirit, He began to do through me what I could not do for myself.

I still needed training and experience to be effective in my work with collegians, but I could trust Christ with all I didn't know. And I could ask for help, admit defeat, and stop hiding my inadequacy. I was free to be who I was and to be honest about where I was in life and Christian maturity.

Once I was honest with God, myself, and others, I began to grow. I was trusting Him and His Word in a new way, and daily I sensed His enabling power in my life. And my ministry began to flourish. I had more appointments than I could handle. My apartment was often packed with students who had come to learn about the Lord. I began to love being in Arizona.

I realized if anything of eternal value was going to be accomplished through me, Christ would have to do it.

I think it is possible that when we present ourselves to God for service, He may look at us with our pride and self-sufficiency and say:

> *I love you, but I need to tear down what is not of My Spirit, so I can build you back up.*
> *I need to wound you so I can heal you.*
> *I see you depending upon your own strength. I see you depending upon yourself. I need to let you experience failure so you will call on Me and depend on Me for your life and strength.*

My feelings told me that it had been a terrible mistake for me to be assigned to Tucson by myself. Yet God had called me there. I came to see that when I trusted in my feelings, I grew more fearful and tried to do things in my own strength. God in His grace showed me that I needed to turn to Him with my fears and put my trust in His Word and His sovereign control. Just as a hot fire melts away impurities in order to strengthen and refine gold, so my experience in Tucson refined my character and strengthened my faith. My assignment at the University of Arizona was God's special way of performing His refining work in my character, His way of beginning to teach me to walk by faith.

But He didn't stop there.

CHAPTER 3

JUST SAY
THE WORD

I poured myself a glass of ice-cold lemonade, sharpened a pencil, and pulled out my legal pad, eager to begin my assignment. Earlier in the day the professor for my summer school Bible course had instructed us, "Bring back to the class a report on everything the book of Romans has to say about faith." It sounded like an easy assignment, one that wouldn't take me long.

But I was in for a surprise. I soon discovered that the word *faith* appears numerous times in Romans and that my study would take longer than I'd thought.

As I read what Romans had to say about faith, I found myself asking, *Faith is probably the most important thing in my life, but how do I define it? What is it?*

My mind flashed back eight years to my time in Tucson right after I'd joined Campus Crusade. Back then I didn't understand a walk of faith. *I've come so far in my understanding,* I thought. But even with all that I'd learned about faith, I realized that I still couldn't define it.

I knew that the Bible made hundreds of references to faith,

such as "The just shall live by faith"[1] and "This is the victory that has overcome the world—our faith."[2] But I was surprised that I couldn't come up with a simple, personalized definition of the word; I had never completed the statement: "For me, faith is _____."

I prayed, *Lord, how would You define faith?*

A story came to mind in which Jesus had told someone, "Not even in Israel have I found such great faith." What was it that Jesus had called "great faith"?

I quickly looked up the passage in Luke 7 about the centurion who was willing to believe that Jesus could heal a loyal and trusted servant who was near death. The centurion told Jesus, "Just say the word, and my servant will be healed."[3] Then the centurion used a personal example to illustrate that he understood what it meant to be taken at his word and obeyed.

In response to the centurion, Jesus turned to the crowd that was following Him and said, "I say to you, not even in Israel have I found such great faith."[4] Jesus seemed to be saying that "great faith" was simply taking Him at His word.

Could this definition be confirmed elsewhere in Scripture? Since Hebrews 11 is often referred to as "faith's hall of fame," I turned there.

After reading and rereading the passage, with all its references to the phrase "by faith," I began to see that all the people mentioned had one thing in common: No matter whom the writer of Hebrews was talking about, each person had simply taken God at His word and obeyed His command. And they were remembered for their faith.

For example, God told Noah to build an ark. Even though it

never had even rained before, Noah took God at His word and built the ark.[5]

God told Abraham to go out to a place that he would receive as an inheritance. Abraham took God at His word, left his familiar surroundings, and he went.[6]

God indicated to Sarah, who was long past the age of childbearing, that she would conceive a son. The Scripture states: "She considered Him faithful who had promised."[7] She took God at His word.

Regardless of the circumstances, despite arguments of logic and reason, and regardless of how he or she felt, each person mentioned in Hebrews 11 believed God and His word and chose to be obedient.

I began to wonder, *If Luke 7 and Hebrews 11 illustrate great faith, is there a passage that illustrates a lack of faith?*

Then I remembered an incident from Mark 4 in which Jesus had just finished a full day of preaching and teaching by the shores of Galilee. He instructed the disciples to go to the other side of the sea. Initially, they took Jesus at His word, got into a boat with Him, and headed for the other side. But when a storm arose, they grew fearful and lost confidence that they would actually reach the shore. When Jesus asked them, "How is it that you have no faith?"[8] He could just as easily have said, "Why are you not taking Me at My word?"

I have always loved the first verse of Mark 5: "And they came to the other side of the sea." Jesus' word proved to be true.

Through my study of these three passages, I had arrived at a simple, workable definition of faith: *Faith is taking God at His word.* I wasn't sure if I would ever have a report on all the book of

Romans says about faith, but I knew that I had learned something that would prove to be very significant in my walk with God.

Still, I had one more question. If faith is a matter of taking God at His word, what does God say about His word? I found the answer in Scripture itself:

"Heaven and earth will pass away, but My words shall not pass away."[9]

"The word of the Lord abides forever."[10]

"The grass withers, the flower fades, but the word of our God stands forever."[11]

These verses were telling me that everything in life may change, but God's Word remains constant. His truth never changes. I was beginning to catch a glimpse of how faith in God's promises could affect me the rest of my life.

For instance, I feel things very deeply. At times I am so happy I think I will never be sad again. Other times I am so sad I think I will never be happy again...and still other times I feel almost nothing.

But as strong and as fluctuating as my feelings are, God's Word is

- truer than anything I feel
- truer than anything I experience
- truer than any circumstance I will ever face
- truer than anything in the world

Why? Because heaven and earth will pass away, but God's Word will not. This means that no matter how I feel or what I experience, I can choose to depend on the Word of God as the unchanging reality of my life.

I look back on that summer evening and that homework

assignment as a turning point in my life. Innumerable times since then, when circumstances and feelings have seemed more real than life itself, I've chosen to believe that God's Word is truer than anything else. I've chosen to walk by faith.

Sometimes that choice has been difficult.

There were times after that summer evening when I didn't feel God's love. I could choose to dwell on that feeling, letting it carry me on into a state of self-pity, or I could say, "Lord, I don't feel loved. That is the truth. That is where I am right now. But, Lord, Your Word says that You love me. In fact, You've said that You have loved me with an everlasting love.[12] You never stop loving me. Your love for me is the one thing that stands when all else has fallen.[13] Your Word says there is no partiality with You.[14] That means You don't love anyone else in the world more than You love me. So, Lord, I thank You that I'm loved. And I'll keep on going, knowing that I am loved by You. Your Word is truer than how I feel."

I began to realize that this kind of response to my feelings gave me the freedom both to be honest with God about my feelings and to choose to believe God's Word when my feelings contradict His promises.

At other times I have felt afraid or lonely or depressed. My heart has literally ached in anguish over the circumstances of life, and in those moments I have been the most tempted to doubt the truth of God's Word. But instead I chose with my will to believe His Word. Thousands of times my prayers have begun, "Lord, I feel…, but, Lord, Your Word says…"

And I've found that He does bring my emotions in line with His Word, in His own timing and in His way.

When I've been tempted to condemn myself for how I feel, it

has helped me to remember that God created us in His image and that part of His image is that we are emotional beings. Feelings aren't wrong. Even Christ had feelings. He didn't "try not to feel." He did not hide His emotions; instead, He took them into His relationship with His Father. He was honest, real, authentic. In the Garden of Gethsemane the night before His crucifixion, Scripture tells us that Jesus was "distressed," "deeply grieved," "troubled," and "in agony."[15] Jesus expressed how He felt and trusted the Father in the midst of His feelings.

We, too, have immeasurable freedom to be candid with the Lord about our feelings, to tell Him honestly where we are and what is going on in our lives.

The Bible promises that, for those of us who truly love God, everything that happens in our lives will have the effect of molding us into Christ's image.[16] Some of us may have prayed a prayer similar to this: "Lord, I pray You'd make me more like You. I pray that You would conform me to the image of Christ." Often, what we really want is for God to give us an anesthetic so we can be unconscious while He performs surgery on our hearts in order to conform us to Christ's perfect character. We don't want to wake up until the transformation is complete! We want the result but not the painful process.

But God doesn't work that way. The Lord is concerned about what we go through, but I believe He is more concerned about how we respond to what we go through. That response is a matter of our wills. He allows the trials, temptations, and pressures of life to come so that we have the opportunity to respond either by trusting our feelings and life experiences or by taking Him at His word.

I have learned to get into the habit of taking God at His

word—and now it is a habit! You and I can either grow accustomed to listening to our feelings, thoughts, and circumstances, letting them control us, or we can be in the habit of taking God at His word despite our feelings and life experiences. We need to choose with our wills to believe that His Word is truer than our feelings.

I have made a lifetime commitment to bank my life on the Word of God, and God has honored that commitment. And yet, there have been times when I could have easily gone back on my commitment because I couldn't believe that anything was truer than what I was going through—times when my feelings have screamed 180 degrees in the opposite direction of God's Word.

In fact, there have been lots of times...

CHAPTER 4

MATTERS OF
CONSCIENCE

One bright August morning as I was dressing for work, I had my television set tuned to NBC's *Today* show. I hadn't been listening closely to the program, but suddenly a newscaster's voice caught my attention as he announced, "Yesterday, Arab and Israeli jets engaged in a confrontation over the Sinai Desert." His next words stunned me: "Evangelist Billy Graham stated last night that he believes Jesus Christ is coming again soon."

I could hardly believe that I'd heard those two announcements one right after the other on national television. The NBC reporter hadn't connected the two incidents, but I had.

Christ's words in Matthew 24 concerning the last days before His second coming flashed into my mind. He said there would be wars, rumors of wars, famines and earthquakes, and false prophets setting out to mislead many. Then He said, "And because lawlessness is increased, most people's love will grow cold."

I stood in the middle of my living room and prayed, "Lord, don't let my love toward You grow cold! Bring revival to our land, our world."

I remembered an old camp slogan, "All fires are the same size at the start." I continued, "You've got to begin somewhere, Lord. So begin with me. If there is anything hindering my relationship with You, please bring it to mind."

That desire and my prayer were tested that very same week.

I was listening to a guest speaker during the summer staff training at Arrowhead Springs, California, then the international headquarters for Campus Crusade. He was talking about the importance of maintaining a clear conscience.

We need to live in such a way, he said, that neither God nor man could point the finger at us and charge, "You've offended me, and you've never tried to make it right." Then he quoted the apostle Paul's declaration: "I also do my best to maintain always a blameless conscience both before God and before men."[1]

His last text was Paul's charge to Timothy to "fight the good fight, keeping faith and a good conscience, which some have rejected and suffered shipwreck in regard to their faith."[2]

The speaker urged us not to become too introspective while examining our conscience, explaining that if something needed to be made right in our relationship with God or someone else, it would surface effortlessly in our minds.

I had never given the subject of a clear conscience much thought until I heard this message. As I sat there, three incidents came clearly and unmistakably to mind. I gulped. *No, Lord. Not that! Or that...or that! You don't mean I have to take care of those!?*

Then I heard the promptings of an inner voice. *Ney, did you mean it when you said you wanted the revival to begin with you?*

Yes.

Do you care more about your reputation with people or with Me?

I care more about my reputation with You.
Ney, are you willing to make things right?
Yes, Lord, I'm willing.

The first experience had to do with my car insurance. Six years earlier I had moved from Tucson to Arrowhead Springs, California, to develop Campus Crusade's human resources department. I had been living on the headquarters grounds and received all my mail there.

Each time my car insurance was due, the insurance company would send me a notice about the amount due and a memo to sign confirming that their information about me was accurate. The last line before the signature space read, "I do not drive more than forty miles weekly to work." The statement had been true—until I moved to the mountains about twenty miles above Arrowhead Springs. My drive to and from work then began averaging almost two hundred miles a week.

When the notice came after my move, I paused as I read the mileage statement: "I do not drive more than forty miles weekly to work."

The wheels of rationalization started clicking in my mind. *I still get my mail here at Arrowhead Springs. Besides, the insurance company doesn't know I've moved, and my premium would probably go up if I told them… I think I'll just sign the memo and send it back.*

Six months later another bill came, along with the memo. I signed it again.

As I remembered what I'd done, I knew my time had come. My stomach felt queasy and weak at the very thought of going to the local agent to confess my actions, but I knew that's what I needed to do. Within a day or so I was on my way.

My hands were clammy as I parked my car in front of the agent's office, a refurbished home built in the 1920s. I had never done anything like this before. Slowly, deliberately I went inside.

As I walked through the door and saw people in the waiting area, my heart sank. I didn't want to tell the whole world my story. My agent looked up and with a friendly smile said, "May I help you?"

"That's okay," I spoke hesitantly. "I don't mind waiting. I'd like to talk with you alone."

When everyone else had gone, he signaled me to follow him into his private office.

I sat down and swallowed hard, perspiration on my brow. "Now, what can I do to help you?" the agent asked.

"This may be one of the most unusual visits you've ever had." I explained to him what I had done, that I realized I had been wrong, and that I had come to make things right by paying back what I owed.

He listened intently as I spoke. As I concluded, his eyes misted with tears.

"Thank you for telling me that, Ney," he said. "Actually, we figure some people overpay and some people underpay, so consider the matter settled."

I couldn't believe what he was saying.

"Are you sure?" I asked. "I'd really be glad to pay whatever I owe."

"No," he replied. "There's really no problem. You don't need to do anything. But I do appreciate your coming. By the way, you work up there with Campus Crusade, don't you?"

"Yes, I do."

He said warmly, "How's Ken Berven? I haven't see him lately."

"He's fine." For several minutes more we talked of the Lord and our mutual faith in Christ. Then I excused myself, thanking him for his time and understanding.

A flood of emotion overwhelmed me as I stepped out into the afternoon sunshine—feelings of joy and relief and a sense of deep inner satisfaction. I had gone to make peace, to right a wrong. I had no idea of how "right" God would make things. "Oh, Lord, thank You," I prayed. "Thank You, thank You for going before me and preparing the way."

The next incident I had to deal with concerned a loan I had recently negotiated at the bank. I had wanted to buy some stock that had just gone on the market. A friend's father was starting a new company and had told me it was certain to be a smashing success. I felt privileged to get in on the ground floor of the new venture.

This is a perfect chance to build up a nest egg for the future, I thought. I dreamed of all the things I could buy for myself and for others as the stock skyrocketed in value. This was sure to be the deal of the century!

However, I had no money to invest in the stock, so I decided to borrow a thousand dollars from my bank. Since my car was nearly paid for, I knew it could be used as equity for the loan.

But when I filled out the forms at the bank, I didn't mention the fact that I would be using the money for investment in stock. I had heard that banks frowned upon loans taken out for something speculative such as stock, and since I didn't want to risk not getting the loan, I wrote "clothes, vacation, and miscellaneous" as the reasons for my request.

As soon as the loan was approved, I rushed downtown to a well-known brokerage firm to purchase my stock. They had no listing for it. A broker I met with begged me not to buy the stock and began offering me alternatives.

But I was determined. I had seen the prospectus, and soon the whole world would know of this progressive new organization. I phoned a broker in the city where the company was located, who sold me the stock at $1.75 a share. Soon it had climbed to $2.50, then $3.00, on up to $4.00 a share. I was elated.

Then, within a week and a half, I received notice from the company that it had come under investigation by the Securities and Exchange Commission. The commission was ordering the stock to be taken off the market immediately. The notice assured me, however, that this was only a temporary condition, and the company would quickly bounce back into competition.

It has never recovered.

Not only did I have to pay back a loan that had become a total financial loss for me, but I also learned that it had indeed been illegal for me to borrow money for the purchase of stock.

Once again I had to right a wrong.

I paid a visit to my loan officer at the bank and explained my story. Even though more than six months had passed since my investment had fallen through, she was, like my insurance agent, amazingly sympathetic and understanding. She said she realized I had probably learned a valuable and expensive lesson—and refused to press any penalties.

And when she learned I would soon be moving to Dallas, Texas, she gave me her business card, suggesting that it might be helpful to use when I opened a new bank account there. She offered to help me in any way possible, even to serve as a reference in future financial transactions!

I left her office exultant and grateful to the Lord for what He had done.

It wasn't until later that I came across these verses in Proverbs: "Hasty speculation brings poverty. Dishonest gain will never last."[3]

My third confession was the most difficult one of all.

The year after I joined the staff, Campus Crusade initiated an Institute of Biblical Studies in order to give the staff in-depth Bible training. That year, one of my courses was in the gospel of John. For the course's final exam, we were given a closed-book, take-home quiz to be completed on our honor.

I clearly remember the afternoon I took the test. I was sitting on a top bunk in my small dorm room, going over the questions. I came to a question that sounded simple enough, but my mind completely blocked on the answer. I was sure I knew the answer, but at that moment I couldn't think of it to save my life.

I began reasoning, *All I need is one clue just to get my mind working again.* I completed all the other questions, then returned to the problem question. But I still couldn't think of the answer.

Then the inward struggle began. *Should I...or shouldn't I?* Back and forth I went. I finally gave in. I opened my Bible and closed it just as quickly. But it was enough to give me the clue I needed for the answer to the question.

I didn't really cheat, I thought as I handed in the exam. *I knew that answer and needed only a little help to recall it.*

But a heaviness slowly began to overtake me that day, and for days following. I confessed my sin to the Lord over and over, but my guilt didn't go away. It became difficult even to look at the gospel of John, much less at the page from which I had sneaked a look.

With the passing of time, my guilt feelings subsided…except for occasions every once in a while when something would remind me. Now, seven years later, I was reminded again. My guilt resurfaced, loud and clear as a clanging bell.

I knew my reputation with people was really on the line this time. It was bad enough to cheat on any test. But a Bible test? It was distasteful to even think about! Again I was faced with the question: Do I care more about my reputation with people or my reputation with the Lord? Was I "willing to be willing" to do the right thing?

I knew this confession could be harder than the other two. I would probably never see the insurance agent or the bank officer again, but to admit my cheating to my professor, a fellow staff member…

That summer the annual all-staff picnic was held in a lovely park in nearby Riverside, California. It was a beautiful day, and there was a festive atmosphere in the air when I arrived. But I didn't have the enthusiasm to enter into the games going on all around. I was thinking about the test.

I told myself that if Ted Martin, the director of the Biblical Studies program, came by I would tell him the whole story. But I was soon headed toward the opposite side of the park away from everyone else, and, finding a secluded spot by a stream, I sat down at a redwood picnic table. I stared for long minutes at the table, then at the trees.

Presently I heard footsteps on an old curved wooden bridge about twenty feet behind me. I wheeled around. Was this a mirage?

Dr. Martin, his wife, Gwen, and their four children were crossing the bridge and heading toward me.

The family came up to the table and greeted me. "Hey, Ney!" Dr. Martin smiled. "What are you doing way over here?"

"Oh, just thinking. Are you on your way to the picnic?"

Dr. Martin replied, "Yes, we were just out exploring, and now we're on our way back."

They started to leave, but I knew this was the time to settle my account.

"Ted," I spoke hesitantly. "Could I talk to you a few minutes before you go?"

"Sure," he said, and the rest of his family kept walking toward the picnic.

With a quivering voice I began, "Ted, something happened seven years ago that I need to tell you about." I related the incident and finished by telling him that I knew I had been wrong and that I was willing to talk to the professor of the course to make things right.

"No," Dr. Martin answered in an understanding voice. "Talking to me is good enough."

He went on, "Ney, we know that things like this go on from time to time. But you're the first person who has ever admitted anything. However, I think you've suffered enough. You don't need to do anything about it."

I gratefully acknowledged his kindness, and as he walked away I felt as though I could have joined the birds in the trees with little effort. Such a weight had been lifted that I practically skipped over to join the picnic, with praise and thanksgiving on my lips.

As I look back on those three confessions, I feel very blessed that each person so warmly received my admission of guilt. My insurance agent could have said, "You owe me several hundred dollars plus penalties and interest." The loan officer could have replied, "I'm afraid we'll have to press charges and take you to court. It will no doubt mean a sizable fine and a possible jail sentence." And Dr. Martin could have said, "I'm afraid you're going to have to retake the course." Even though I feared the worst, I knew I had to take the initiative to make things right.

And it wasn't the *measure* of wrong that determined whether I should deal with my different circumstances. The situations I encountered may seem minor to others. Obviously if I had robbed a bank, shoplifted, or aimed a pistol at someone, I would eventually have to face up to my actions. The fact that I committed wrongdoing, however minor, was enough to warrant efforts toward reconciliation.

I had asked God to bring to my mind anything that might be hindering my relationship with Him, and those three things surfaced. I've prayed the same prayer many times since, and at times nothing surfaces. But when something does come up, I like to use what has been called the Christian's bar of soap. First John 1:9 states, "If we confess our sins, He is faithful and righteous to *forgive* us our sins and to *cleanse* us from *all* unrighteousness" (emphasis mine.) So I pull out a piece of paper and write down issues or sins that I want to bring before the Lord. Once I have confessed those sins, I claim His promise of forgiveness and cleansing. I can do this because He says, "If we ask anything according to His will, He hears us. And if we know that He hears us in whatever we ask, we know that we have the requests which we have asked from

Him."[4] On the basis of God's Word—not our feelings—we can claim His righteousness and cleansing and continue to walk in His victory.

Revival had begun in me. I had taken care of the three things God had brought to my mind. My conscience was clear in every relationship I could think of…or was it?

There was one I had forgotten.

CHAPTER 5

A CHANGE
OF HEART

Early one morning the phone rang. It was my mother calling.

In her Southern manner she began, "Honey, your daddy and I were talking this week, and he told me how proud he is of each of you children. 'I can't tell them myself,' he said, 'but I'd like for you to call each one of them and tell them for me how proud I am of them.'"

This was the call of a lifetime.

"Mother, he really said that?"

"Yes, he did."

"Will you say it for me the way he said it? Don't leave out a word."

"Your daddy wanted me to call and tell you how proud he is of you."

"Mother, will you say it just one more time?"

"Your daddy wanted me to call and tell you he is proud of you."

"Would you please tell him 'thank you' for me and that this is the best present I've ever received in all my life?"

I hung up the phone, elated and grateful for how God had healed this relationship.

It had all started with an incident when I was six years old. I was barely three feet tall, standing on the edge of the municipal pool. "Jump, Ney Ann!" coaxed my dad, his arms outstretched. "I'll catch you!"

He was standing in water that was over my head. I was petrified to jump in and, trembling, called out, "No, I can't do it!"

"Yes, you can," he shouted. "Jump, and I'll catch you!"

I finally jumped…but my father didn't catch me. My head went under the water, and I came up sputtering and thrashing. Daddy had moved away from the edge of the pool, hoping I would swim to him.

I began to cry, "Daddy, you moved! You said you wouldn't!"

His response crushed me. He laughed and said, "Ney Ann, you've gotten upset over nothing. You know I wouldn't let anything happen to you. I was just trying to teach you to swim."

That experience had a devastating effect on my six-year-old mind. I had trusted my father with everything that my little heart could muster—and he had let me down. He'd said he would catch me, but he didn't.

Some of the deepest hurts we'll ever know come from those we care most about and often result in bruised relationships within our families. And those relationships are often the hardest to heal. As I grew older, that experience in the pool became representative of others I had with my father, and by the time I entered college, my bitterness toward him was full grown and deeply rooted.

But I didn't give our relationship a lot of thought until I attended a meeting where a staff member said some things that got my attention.

I knew that the Bible says, "God is love."[1] I also knew that 1 Corinthians 13 reveals what love is. But the speaker said one thing that was like bright sunshine piercing a long-closed dungeon: "If God is love, and 1 Corinthians 13 tells what love is, then God loves you and God loves me with that same kind of love."

I had never heard this before.

I had heard that I was supposed to love *other* people with a 1 Corinthians 13 kind of love. I had also been told to test my own love for others by inserting my name each time the chapter mentions love. (I had failed the test!) But it hadn't occurred to me to put God's name with the word *love*.

When I did, I discovered that:

God's love toward me is kind,

God's love toward me is patient,

God's love toward me is not provoked,

God's love toward me does not take into account a wrong
    suffered,

God's love toward me would bear all things,
    believe all things,
    hope all things,
    endure all things.

God's love toward me would never fail.

It was overwhelming to think God loved me in that way.

As I drove home from the meeting, I began to think of my father. I thought of how we had been at odds with each other most of my growing-up years. I knew it was not unusual for a teenager to have conflicts with her parents. That was normal enough. But my conflict with my dad seemed far beyond the norm.

I thought back to the earliest years of my life when my father had been a struggling law student. Those were the post-Depression years, and he studied long and hard during the hours he wasn't working to help make ends meet. He had very little time to spend with me, and by the time I entered first grade, I hardly knew him. As a result, the major influence in my life was my mother, whom I adored.

As the years flew by and I grew older, I became afraid of my dad. When he raised his voice at my mother or me, something in me shuddered. This fear turned to hostility during my teenage years. My friends' fathers seemed to care about the things they did and the awards they received, but my father was so caught up in his own interests that I felt he didn't care about what happened to me. I knew he loved his work, but I felt insignificant to him.

In high school and college my hostility turned to a subtle rebellion. I thought, *You go your way, and I'll go mine. You don't bother me, and I won't bother you.* If Dad yelled at me, I yelled back at him in my heart, but I was too fearful to yell aloud. If he ignored me, I ignored him. If he hurt my feelings, I'd try to hurt his. I wanted to give him what I thought he deserved.

Daddy and I rarely communicated. The only way he seemed able to express his love for me was by giving me things. But that's not what I longed for from my father, so his actions didn't feel like love, and since I couldn't feel his love for me, I began to wonder if he really did love me.

I had been waiting all those years for him to love me in the way that I wanted to be loved. When he didn't, my hatred and resentment grew.

Then I heard the message on God's love. If God is love and 1 Corinthians 13 describes God's love, then it meant that

God's love toward my dad is kind,

God's love toward my dad is patient,

God's love toward my dad is not provoked,

God's love toward my dad does not take into account wrongs
  suffered,

God's love toward my dad would bear all things,
    believe all things,
    hope all things,
    endure all things.

God's love toward my dad would never fail.

I thought, *If God loves my father just the way he is, who am I not to love him also?* My love had been conditional, based on my father's performance. My love had said, "Daddy, I'll love you if you do this and if you do that." Yet God's love simply said, "I love you, period." No ifs about it.

It was as though God were saying to me, "I love you just the way you are. I love him just the way he is. I want you to love him just the way he is."

Tears streamed down my face as I drove up the mountain road to my home after the meeting. For the first time in my life I decided to accept my father just as he was. As I reflected on his background and childhood, I was able to see that he had just given to me out of what had been given to him.

Dad was an only child, raised in a small town north of Shreveport, Louisiana. His parents began having marital difficulty early in his life and soon separated and divorced. He stayed with his mother. She died when he was thirteen years old, a great loss to a young boy.

Dad went to live with an aunt and uncle. In the meantime, his father was away most of the time, dabbling in oil and investments, making and losing tens of thousands of dollars. He rarely expressed love for his son verbally or emotionally, but he did so materially—demonstrating his care by buying his son gifts and taking him on occasional trips. I could see this pattern repeated years later in the way my father related to his own family.

On the other hand, my mother was the youngest of four daughters, raised on a wheat farm in the small community of Jet, near the Oklahoma panhandle, where her parents had pioneered the land. Love and closeness characterized her family. They shared such activities as daily farm chores, recreation, harvesting, and church.

My mother's family emotionally and verbally expressed their appreciation for one another and demonstrated their love through hugs and kisses and many acts of kindness. And my mother carried over this pattern as she raised her own family. She kept detailed diaries of my first three years of life, until my twin brother and sister were born—what I did, what I ate, the words I spoke, and how much I weighed. She was always available to take me anywhere I needed to go and was always ready with words of encouragement for my achievements, however small.

As a child, I had concluded these many differences between my parents meant "Mother loves me and Daddy doesn't." But now I could see that they both loved me as best they knew how in light of their particular backgrounds.

I was grateful for this new understanding. It seemed as if God had done something new in my life. But I knew the real test was yet to come.

Two months later I flew home to Louisiana for vacation, still filled with an attitude of love for and acceptance of my dad. I found I was free from judging him, criticizing him, or expressing disapproval either verbally or nonverbally.

I remember one day in particular. We were sitting in the living room together. I was on the couch, and Daddy was in his reclining chair in front of the television. Soon he fell asleep. I looked over at him in his chair for a long time and then said in a soft whisper, "Daddy, I love you, and I accept you just as you are, sitting there in your chair."

Over the next few days, a strange thing began to happen. As he felt my acceptance, my father began to respond with warmth. He seemed to be more caring and sensitive to little things he could do for me. For example, he came with me to the doctor's office when I had to have minor surgery. He waited for me and bought the prescribed medicine at the nearby pharmacy. There was a dress shop near his law office. He brought home three dresses on approval so that I could choose which ones I wanted to keep.

God was beginning to restore our relationship!

Soon I began to run across verses in Scripture that spoke of parents and of their children's relationships to them. "He chooses our inheritance for us,"[2] and He wove "me in my mother's womb."[3] And "For this reason, I bow my knees before the Father, from whom every family in heaven and on earth derives its name."[4] God had chosen my parents for me! He was not surprised that I was born into my particular family. When I realized this truth, I thanked God for my parents—for the first time in my life.

It wasn't until several years later that I read a verse in Ephesians with new meaning. "Honor your father and mother (which is the first commandment with a promise), that it may be well with you, and that you may live long on the earth."⁵ I discovered that the word *honor* means "to count precious, to prize, to value."

I prayed, "Lord, will You show me how to honor my parents? I really want to. Will You give me creativity and show me what to do?"

The Lord answered my prayer in definite ways.

Usually when I went home for a visit, I spent the majority of my time with all my friends and very little time at home. One of the first thoughts that came to me in answer to my prayer was that the next time I went home, I should spend some time with my parents before I started visiting my friends.

Also, on my very next visit, I noticed that my mother and dad's bedroom furniture, though perfectly good, had nearly twenty years of wear and tear. *Wouldn't it be great to redo their bedroom furniture?* I thought.

They gave me their permission, so I sanded down the bed, the dressers, the nightstand, and the bookcase and refinished the furniture with an antique effect. Mother and I found some beautiful fabric and reupholstered their headboard and made matching decorator pillows. They loved the results and couldn't get over the fact that I had given four or five days to a project—just for them.

I also thought, *When was the last time I gave my parents a present for no reason…just to say, "I love you, and I'm thinking of you?"* I couldn't remember the last time. We usually exchanged gifts on birthdays and Christmas. But my excitement over getting them gifts for no reason began to grow.

My parents have always loved to cook. So, acting on my desire to get them a special surprise, I stopped at a roadside vegetable stand and bought a huge grocery bag full of black-eyed peas. With Mother and Dad watching, almost awestruck, I sat in the living room shelling peas for hours. They were delighted with the gift, and my father, who was an excellent cook, took unusual pleasure in specially preparing them for us to eat.

Another time, when I was visiting the University of Missouri campus in Columbia, one morning I walked by some shops on the way to the student union building. An item in a jewelry store window caught my eye—a sterling silver necklace engraved with the letters ALBERTA. My mother's name!

I went inside the shop.

"How much is that necklace in the window—the silver one on the far right?" I asked. The salesclerk behind the counter said, "Well, it's so much per letter and takes approximately six weeks for delivery."

"I don't want to order one," I replied. "I'd like the one in the window. My mother's name is Alberta."

She seemed a little surprised, "My name is Alberta! The company wanted to make a sample necklace, so I gave them my name to engrave. But I suppose I could sell it to you." My mother loved her unique gift.

My father loved to fish, and our family has always enjoyed fishing trips to nearby lakes. Once, when he and I went fishing, I took a picture of him holding a very tiny fish he had caught, a big grin on his round, Jackie Gleason–type face. I had the picture enlarged

FAITH IS NOT A FEELING

and framed and sent it to his law office as a surprise. Delighted, he took it to the courthouse to show some of his colleagues. It remained in a prominent place in his office for years.

Sometime later I had to make a major career decision. The thought came to me, *Would I be willing to go to my father and seek his advice?* I also wanted to ask his forgiveness for some of my actions and bad attitudes of years gone by. We had never talked much about personal things, so it was a bit scary to me.

One Sunday afternoon when I was visiting my family, Dad and I were at home watching a football game together. I mustered up all the courage I could. Then I asked him for counsel on my career decision. He was extremely helpful, and the conversation went much better than I had expected.

Then I said, "Daddy, there's something else I've been thinking about. I harbored a lot of bad attitudes when I was growing up, attitudes of ungratefulness and lack of love. I realize how wrong I was, and I'd like to ask you to forgive me. Will you forgive me?"

He turned in his large, overstuffed reclining chair and looked at me with a slight twinkle in his eyes. "No." Then he paused. "I don't remember all those things, except for the time..." He named an instance and laughed.

I thought a moment and said, "Well, will you forgive me for the things you can remember?"

"Yes," he answered.

The ball game continued.

I told him that I'd been invited to go on a guided tour to Israel—my first. I wanted to know what he thought.

He replied in Archie Bunker fashion, "I wouldn't give you a nickel for the Wailing Wall. But if you want to go, it's okay with me."

Then I said, "Daddy, I think I'll drive back to Dallas and listen to the rest of the game on the radio."

"Fine," he said. "That's a good idea. You'll beat some of the traffic."

We got up out of our chairs. "Now, where are you going on your next trip?" He had never asked me that before.

"Houston and Nacogdoches," I replied.

"Why don't you warm up one of those cheeseburgers from last night to eat on the way back?" he asked.

I wasn't sure how hungry I was for a leftover cheeseburger, but I wasn't about to turn it down. "Good idea!" I said.

I gathered my things to leave. At the door he handed me the cheeseburger and asked, "When will you be home next?" He had never asked me that before either.

"Oh, about the twenty-first or twenty-second."

Smiling, he said, "I'll see you on the twenty-first."

A couple of days later I talked to my mother on the phone. "Did Daddy say anything to you about our visit?" I asked.

"Yes, he said, 'Ney must be losing her mind! She asked me for some advice.'"

Sometime later I read a passage in Proverbs that I thought about for a long time.

> Listen, my son, to your father's instruction
> and do not forsake your mother's teaching.
> They will be a garland to grace your head
> and a chain to adorn your neck.[6]

My parents had never sat me down and taught or instructed me as such. And yet, as I thought about the passage, I realized that they had actually instructed me through their actions, through how they lived their lives. I began to write down on a legal pad what I had learned from my parents, the things I appreciated about them, and the qualities they had helped build into my life.

My thoughts evolved into a five-page letter that I sent to my folks on their wedding anniversary. The letter contained the words that I might someday wish that I had said to them. When Mother and Dad received my letter, it touched them so deeply that they sat down on the bed and cried.

Parents need and want to know that their children appreciate all they have done for them through the years. They need to know that we have grateful spirits, that they have worth in our eyes, and that we value their counsel and accept them as they are, though they may be different from us.

God wants to heal broken and strained relationships, ones filled with tension and lacking love. In the beginning I certainly didn't feel like showing love to my father. Doing so was an act of faith. And though my father never asked me to forgive him of anything, the Lord asked that of me. And through it all He changed my heart and deepened my understanding of faith.

Once I invited God to deal with my hostility, I began to see my father's many wonderful qualities to which I had previously been blind. He was dear, funny, and thoughtful. My friends loved him and thought he was a marvelous storyteller. He was also a gifted lawyer—and a great man in my eyes. Today, whenever I think of him, my heart fills with love and appreciation.

In many ways my father never changed. But I did. And that has made all the difference.

CHAPTER 6

A BRICK
AT A TIME

Relationships can be full of pain or blessing. And many times they are a mixture of both the heights and depths—at one time being a source of supreme joy, and at another, excessive sorrow. They teach us much about who we are and how we may need to change.

In 1969 I found myself in a relationship that would prove to be one of the most significant of my life.

After six years of managing the human resources department, I assumed the responsibility of traveling to college campuses throughout the south central states. My job was to meet with staff and students at various schools and provide them with spiritual leadership and training. Although representatives normally traveled alone, I asked to be part of a team. My request was honored, and Jean Pietsch and I became partners.

Because we would be working so closely together, Jean and I decided to share an apartment. Our living arrangement started out beautifully. We made a commitment to each other to have a transparent, open, walls-down, roof-off relationship. We determined to "walk in the light"[1] with the Lord and with one another and to communicate with one another—whether or not we felt like it.

We sat down and talked about our personal likes, dislikes, and preferences—something I'd come to call "preventive maintenance." The company that manufactured my car had a preventive maintenance program to encourage owners to bring in their cars periodically to catch problems before they happened. I had found this practice, in principle, to be extremely profitable in new living situations as well. I'd learned from past experience that if two people don't take care of problems a brick at a time, they will build a wall between them. And the wall will either remain there forever or come crashing down in some traumatic way. The two alternatives can be equally painful.

As Jean and I talked, I learned that she was a meticulous housekeeper and wanted things as neat and tidy as possible. She learned that I hated the sound of chewing gum popping. It affects me much like the sound of chalk screeching across a blackboard! I disliked the fact that gum smacking bothered me so much, but Jean agreed to honor my feelings, and I determined to respect her preferences.

We also committed to pray, both with and for each other. Our home base was Dallas, Texas, and the day we moved in together, we knelt and prayed, "Lord, we are Yours. We commit ourselves to You and to each other, for You to do in and through us all that You desire. Whatever happens, Father, don't let us fall short of experiencing the fullness of Your purposes."

We asked God to make our relationship a reflection of Christ's prayer in John 17, in which He asked the Father that His followers might be perfected in unity, becoming one even as Christ and the Father are one. In my mind, unity or oneness did not mean that we had to be identical people, alike in every way. Rather it meant that we would not allow conflicts, hostilities, and resentments to be sustained and to serve as bricks that could form a wall in our relationship. Jean and I would be different from each other, but our relationship would be harmonious, just as musical instruments can blend although they come in every variety.

So we established our relationship on principles that we found in God's Word, on prayer, and on a commitment to communicate. But we knew little about our different backgrounds and emotional makeup.

As weeks passed, I began feeling increasingly uncomfortable around Jean. Her manner seemed cold, a strange combination of hostility and indifference. She didn't express these things so much verbally as she did in attitudes that seemed to come from within, from her spirit.

Jean was a very gifted person and a self-described loner. Because of her talents and abilities, she always rose quickly to the top and wasn't able to establish equal relationships with those around her. She was always in leadership positions over her peers. I later discovered that our friendship was her first sustained peer relationship. Our relationship was the first to provide her with an opportunity to work out personal problems with someone on a consistent basis.

I tried to understand Jean's behavior in light of what I knew about her background, but I still felt at a loss as to how to respond to her. Despite our intentions, it seemed that the brick wall we had determined not to build was under construction. I had always been a "people person." Throughout high school and college, I majored more in people than in my studies. I savored each opportunity to know and enjoy all kinds of people, but I wasn't always sure how to relate to Jean.

Our greatest source of frustration stemmed from the different ways we approached communication. Jean seemed continually threatened by my openness in expressing feelings and reactions, and she'd often withdraw simply out of retaliation. In turn, I sometimes would be hurt and discouraged. Despite some growth in mutual understanding, our differences wore on both of us over a period of time.

On days when tension filled the air of our apartment, I escaped and took a break at a neighborhood coffee shop. Often I sat there for what seemed like a very long time, staring out the window. *How did I get myself into this mess?* I would think. *Living with someone who seems so hostile, so cold, so controlled and unfeeling.*

My frequent retreats to the coffee shop helped me regain a balance in my perspective. Because of the tension between Jean and me, I had been finding it easy to question God's wisdom and sovereignty in placing us together. I was tempted to think, *We just can't expect to get along because we are so different.*

But when I could get away from home and think, I would remember that my frame of reference should be what God's Word said, not what I was experiencing at home. I thought of Jesus' words when He exposed Satan as the one who "comes only to steal, and kill, and destroy"[2] the abundant life Christ has provided for us. As I sat in the coffee shop, God's perspective would flood my mind. I knew that He had called Jean and me together. And since Jesus had prayed for our oneness, it could only be Satan who was out to destroy it. As I remembered to place my faith in God's

Word, I was able to look past my frustrations with Jean to the Lord Himself. When I headed back to the apartment, I always felt a little better.

On one occasion, as I came in the front door, Jean looked up. "How was your outing?" she asked.

"Fine," I answered. "I ran some errands and then went to the coffee shop."

"You really like that place, don't you?"

I paused. "Yes, I do. It's a good place to collect my thoughts." Then I said, "Jean, did you feel the tension in the air that I felt when I left?"

"Yes, I did," she replied.

"Do you know what caused it?"

Jean paused this time, pensive and thoughtful. "No, Ney, I don't know exactly where my feelings come from. Can we pray about it...again?"

And so we repeated a practice that would prove to be the glue that held our relationship together over the next three intense, important years. We knelt beside the living room couch and prayed. "Lord, we don't particularly feel like praying, but here we are. Your Word says we should always pray and not faint.[3] And we feel like fainting, so we'd better pray! Your Word also says, 'In every thing give thanks: for this is the will of God in Christ Jesus concerning [us].'[4] So while we are in this, we choose with our wills to thank You for what we are going through together, even though we don't fully understand our struggles.

"Thank You for Your promise that all things—including this—will work together for good to those who love You, and we do, and who are called according to Your purpose, and we are.[5]

You've also said that in You there is no darkness at all,[6] so we ask You to shed light on our paths and give us wisdom and understanding.

"We claim Your victory over Satan in our lives. We pray for the oneness You want us to have. And, Lord, Your Word says that we are in the process of being conformed to the image of Christ.[7] We ask You not to stop with us until You are finished. Even though it is painful, we want You to carry on Your work in our lives to accomplish Your purpose."

Once again the tension dissolved, and a spirit of unity returned.

Jean and I knew how different we were emotionally. But when we couldn't meet on any other level, we knew we could meet in Jesus Christ. We could meet at the foot of the cross. We could meet spiritually in prayer, and we did, hundreds of times while we lived together.

Our differences provided thousands of opportunities for each of us either to allow bricks to form walls in our relationship or to deal with those barriers day by day, one at a time. Sometimes these opportunities arose out of the mundane, practical experiences of everyday life.

For instance, for forty-five years my father took coffee to my mother while she was still in bed—a thoughtful gesture to help her begin her mornings. And when I was home visiting, my parents would usually bring coffee to me in the mornings.

So I started taking Jean her coffee every morning. But one morning I noticed that, rather than being glad about it, she seemed extremely tense and uncomfortable.

I paused, puzzled. *Maybe I'm doing the wrong thing,* I thought.

A knot began to form in my stomach. I knew we needed to talk.

Later I asked, "Jean, would you rather I not bring you coffee every morning?" As we discussed it, Jean said, "Ney, I think I'm embarrassed and uncomfortable because I didn't think of doing it first. I feel unworthy of receiving your act of kindness because I hadn't thought of doing it for you, which also makes me uncomfortable thanking you for it."

Years later she told me, "Your simple gesture was the beginning of innumerable incidents that revealed to me just how insecure and proud I was. I had the mistaken idea that I had to know everything, think of everything, and do everything or I was unworthy! I put myself under a lot of pressure, didn't I?"

Our first trip together took us to Lubbock, Texas. One morning we went to the grocery store to buy some things for breakfast. As we were looking over the frozen orange juice selection, I asked Jean, "Which kind would you like?"

She immediately tensed and seemed completely unable to answer my question. That familiar knot began forming in my stomach. I could almost feel another brick being laid.

Later I asked if we could talk about what had happened at the grocery store. Jean answered, "Well, once again, I was uncomfortable with your thoughtfulness. I would have expected you to choose the juice without asking my opinion. I'm just not used to such detailed concern and care."

"Jean, I don't want to be a pressure to you, but I do care about your feelings and preferences."

She replied, "God is the One who chooses to let us be a pressure on other people, Ney. And He is able to take the pressure off whenever He chooses. In the meantime, we can ride it out and hopefully benefit from it, so please, don't stop expressing that thoughtfulness to me. It's helping me break down some barriers inside."

Another time, I had to learn to be on the receiving end. Because of moving and settling-in expenses, I had an extremely dry spell financially. When my paycheck would come, it would already be spoken for, with little left over even for the bare necessities.

Never before had I needed to be dependent on anyone for such things as shampoo, hair spray, even Scotch tape. I hated to borrow from Jean, but I thought I had little choice.

I sensed, however, that it was as hard on her to give to me as it was for me to borrow, which made the situation difficult for both of us.

One day I said, "Jean, I really hate to have to ask you for these things, but I don't know what else I can do. And my asking seems to be hard on you."

She told me that, having grown up with three sisters, each of whom had their own things, she rarely had to share personal items, and that practice had carried over to her roommate relationships. "I know I'm being selfish. I think the Lord wants to teach me to be more giving," she said.

I said, "Well, it's easy for me to give, but very difficult for me to receive! God must be wanting to teach me to receive."

We were able to laugh together, recognizing God's providence in teaching us opposite principles through the same situation.

In time our communication improved. We learned to put each issue on an imaginary table between us and to discuss it objectively. Jean would share with me her perspective of a particular incident, then I would do the same.

We discovered that we normally approached the same thing from opposite directions, but the more frequently we discussed our perspectives, the greater our understanding of one another became. Sometimes we would gain insight just by talking things out. If need be, one of us would ask the other's forgiveness. Those times when we could not come to an understanding, we simply agreed to leave the issue on the table.

Often we gained objectivity by asking ourselves, "Is this conflict like any others I've had previously?" Sometimes our reactions sprang from similar experiences in the past rather than the present situation. This likely was the case if we found ourselves reacting far beyond what the present situation merited.

Once, when Jean and I discussed this question, we discovered that I reminded her in some ways of other people she had known, people whom she had resented because of their freedom to be emotionally expressive. As Jean told me about these emotionally difficult relationships, my heart was full of compassion for her and what she had been through. It helped give me insight and understanding regarding some of the tensions we had experienced.

We also learned to deal with what I've come to call a "vain imagination balloon." A vain imagination can occur when (1) I think you're thinking something negative about me or (2) you think I'm thinking something negative about you. Usually a vain imagination has no firm basis in reality. In other words, the thought hasn't been verbalized, and it is not a known fact. For example, someone might think,

I don't think she likes me.
He wishes I would leave.
She doesn't like my hair.

He thinks I'm not dressed properly.

We imagine such thoughts to be true, and so they "balloon" in our minds, floating in and out and negatively affecting our relationship. Vain imaginations can be very destructive. Many relationships have been destroyed simply because the individuals involved believed their imaginings without checking to see if they were true.

Jean and I agreed to take care of this brick by discussing openly any vain imagination one of us had about the other. Because we told each other what we thought the other was thinking, we were able to put needles in our balloons—and they disappeared!

We had the opportunity to "deflate a balloon" during a visit to Kansas University. One afternoon we were preparing for some evangelistic meetings in a sorority house. My heart was very heavy because I felt, based on her behavior that day, that Jean really didn't want to be around anyone, especially me. I thought, *I just can't go into those meetings until I've talked it over with her.*

Just before it was time to go to the meeting, I mustered up the courage to talk to her about my impressions. "Jean," I asked, "can we talk before we go?"

She looked up from her book and said, "Sure."

I continued, "I have a strong feeling that you don't want to go to this meeting with me tonight."

She exclaimed, "Oh, no, Ney! That never occurred to me. But I was thinking that you didn't want to go to the meeting with me!"

"Jean, I promise, that never even occurred to me!" Both of us were visibly relieved, knowing that Satan was truly at work to kill, steal, and destroy our unity, especially when we were about to speak at the meetings.

Because of our very different backgrounds, Jean and I entered our relationship with different expectations. Wrong expectations can be another cause of problems in relationships. We can come to demand more of people than they are capable of giving, or we may simply begin to take them for granted.

For example, I once heard the story of a man who decided to try an experiment for one month. In this experiment he planned to go up and down a certain neighborhood block and give one-hundred-dollar bills to each household as a gift, with no strings attached.

On the first day of his experiment, as he went from house to house, the residents seemed extremely suspicious—of his sanity. They would hesitantly reach from behind their screen doors and then quickly grab the bills. They reacted similarly on the second day of his rounds.

But by the third and fourth days, many of the people had spent the bills and found them to be the real thing. The neighborhood was buzzing with the news of these daily gifts of hundred-dollar bills.

The second week people were actually waiting on their front porches, peering down the street as they watched for the man to come. They began visiting with one another, shouting in neighborly fashion across yards and the street.

By the third week, however, the novelty of the man's visits seemed to be wearing off. The residents had a humdrum attitude toward the daily gifts. The gifts were becoming old hat. By the fourth week, when the pattern of visits had become firmly established, they were considered an accepted part of everyday neighborhood life.

On the last day of the month the man tried a different approach. He walked down the street again but with no money to give away. As he did so, a strange thing happened. Residents threw open their doors, stepped out on their porches, and shouted angrily, "Where's our money?" and "You so-and-so, how dare you not give me my hundred dollars today!"

What had happened? The people had come to expect and even demand something that was originally presented to them as an unmerited gift. They had grown to feel that the man owed them the money.

We can be the same way with other people and with God. All of life—our families, our friends, our material possessions, our health—starts out as a gift. As life goes on, we can begin to take those gifts for granted and develop expectations of how things are supposed to be. If and when the gifts are withdrawn, we may become angry or demanding because we think we have a right to them. Instead, we would be wise to determine to be grateful for whatever is given to us.

Romans 15:7 beautifully expresses the principle of accepting others as gifts: "Wherefore, accept one another, just as Christ also accepted us to the glory of God." God is actually glorified when we accept one another, and we dishonor Him when we don't.

If we do not choose to accept others, then we will demand that they perform according to our wishes. If others meet our expectations, we usually have few problems with them. But when they don't perform as we expect, then we tend to become judgmental toward them. We let them know in various ways that they have fallen short of our standards, and they begin to feel they are failures in our eyes.

David writes in Psalm 62 that his hopes and expectations were in God alone. Why? Because God is the only constant in life; everything else is variable. If we put our hopes in variables, we'll invariably be disappointed.

When I was living with Jean, I often had to ask myself, "Where have I placed my hopes? In Jean's performance or in the Lord?" If we plant our hopes in another person's performance, or even our own, our lives will become a roller-coaster ride simply because people's performances go up and down.

Though all of these things—individual differences, vain imaginations, and wrong expectations—can contribute to problems in relationships, perhaps the most destructive force of all is that of hurt. At times the differences between Jean and me caused tremendous pain.

I remember vividly one evening when Jean wasn't home. I knelt beside my bed, crying out in prayer, "Lord, I don't feel like Jean loves me, and I don't feel any love for her. After all these years I thought I knew something about love, but I'm not sure I really do.

"I pray that You would teach me about Your love. I've run out of mine. I yield my body to You as an instrument of righteousness. I pray that I can be to Jean what she needs from You, and only You know what that is. By Your Spirit, please do for me and through me what I cannot do for myself."

I knew that both of our hearts were right and that we both loved the Lord. We were different, but different didn't mean one of us was "wrong." But when I was hurt by those differences, I responded in a variety of ways.

My first tendency was to blame Jean or find fault with her. I would think, *If it weren't for Jean, everything would be all right.* But then I would take hold of my thoughts and choose with my will not to blame her. I had to take personal responsibility for my behavior and for the negative attitudes that surfaced in my heart.

For example, I would pray, "Lord, what qualities are You wanting to build into my life through this experience?" Since I was finding it difficult to love Jean, the answer that came to mind was "love."

As I began to dwell on 1 Corinthians 13, I was once again reminded that God's kind of love has a lot more to do with the will than it does with feelings and emotions. God's Word says that we should not judge others. It tells us that He sees the beginning and the end and that He knows where each of us has come from. He sees all the hurt we've experienced.

Once a little boy and his father were riding together on a train. All day long the boy sniffed and whined and cried intermittently. When night fell, the boy and his father retired to a sleeping berth on the train. But the boy's sobbing could be heard through the curtains. A fellow passenger, who had been hearing the little boy's crying for hours, became impatient and irritated. In disgust, he jumped from his berth to the floor and threw back the curtains where father and son were settled in for the night.

He said harshly, "Mister, if you can't control this boy and make him stop crying, you need to let his mother handle him."

The father replied softly, "Sir, his mother has just passed away. We are taking her home to be buried."

The observer had seen only part of the truth and had judged the whole. When he gained additional information, he could understand the behavior.

In the same way, we can trust that if we saw the whole picture—people's entire background and life experiences—we would better understand their behavior. We can choose to love instead of to judge when someone hurts us.

When another person causes us pain, we often want to retaliate. We want vengeance, and this can destroy any relationship. But God's Word says, "Let all be harmonious, sympathetic, brotherly, kindhearted, and humble in spirit; not returning evil for evil, or insult for insult, but giving a blessing instead."[8] We need to practice giving a blessing when we've been hurt.

Jean and I learned to give each other a blessing by sowing good seeds into each other's life.

For example, I once had a garden, and I discovered that when I planted a cucumber seed, for example, the seed didn't yield just one cucumber, but many. Not only that, if I planted cucumber seeds, I reaped cucumbers, not carrots. I got exactly what I sowed—and even more than I sowed. The same thing is true of our actions.

When we hear that someone has reaped negative consequences from their wrong actions, we often respond, "You reap what you sow." But this principle also holds true in the context of doing good things that reap good consequences. Sowing bad seeds can reap difficulties, but sowing good seeds can reap love and harmony. Galatians 6:7-9 says, "Do not be deceived, God is not mocked; for *whatever a man sows, this he will also reap.* For the one who sows to his own flesh shall from the flesh reap corruption, but the one who sows to the Spirit shall from the Spirit reap eternal life. *And let us not lose heart in doing good, for in due time we shall reap if we do not grow weary*" (emphasis mine).

James 3:18 indicates that if we want to make peace, we must sow righteous seed. What is righteous seed? It is the fruit of the Spirit; it is Christlike behavior and a Christlike response to any given situation. Galatians 5 describes the fruit of the Spirit as "love, joy, peace, patience, kindness, goodness, faithfulness, gentleness, self-control; against such things there is no law."[9] That means we can be as loving, kind, patient, and good as we want to be, because there's no law against it!

When someone sends a "hate seed" my way, I can let it take root and grow a larger crop of hatred and then throw seeds from it back into the other person's life. In turn, that hate seed will produce more hate seeds and even more resentment and bitterness. Or I can acknowledge the seed for what it is but refuse to retaliate and can instead break the cycle by forgiving and doing good to the other person.

Jean and I did our best to sow good seed into one another's lives. Our first year together was by far our most difficult, yet during that year I secretly saved mementos from each one of our trips. I saved postcards, souvenirs, and pictures and kept a log of our ministry. At the end of the year, I put it all together in a large scrapbook and surprised her with it.

On the other hand, Jean would often make our airline reservations, cook great meals for us, and write or phone ahead to make arrangements for our trips. There were times when neither of us felt like doing nice things for the other, but in these ways we chose to sow good seed into each other's life.

Perhaps the greatest healing response to hurt, however, is forgiveness. I decided to choose with my will to forgive Jean whenever I felt hurt by her. I had to practice forgiveness over and over again. One thing that helped was to break down the word *forgive* and ask, "Am I looking *for* a way of *giving* to Jean?" or "Am I withholding something from her?" If I found that I was withholding in my heart, then I really didn't have an attitude of *forgiveness,* and I wasn't looking *for* ways of *giving* to her.

I've also asked myself, "Is my God bigger than my hurt?"

I am the one to choose whether to allow God to loom larger in my eyes than the hurt I've experienced. Or I can allow the hurt to become the all-consuming issue in my life, so that it becomes impossible to see God in the situation. It is often difficult to choose to see God as being larger than my hurt, but ultimately it is the right choice. And it was the right choice for me in my relationship with Jean.

In our three years of working together, Jean and I traveled to university campuses in Texas, Louisiana, Oklahoma, Kansas, Missouri, Nebraska, Colorado, and Wyoming. We spoke hundreds of times, saw people come to know Christ as Savior, and saw many lives changed. Because we chose to honor the Lord and each other, I believe that God used us as a team in many special ways.

Jean and I lived together, ate together, ministered, entertained and worked through problems together. As time passed, we began to catch glimpses of true oneness.

The psalmist wrote, "How good and how pleasant it is for brethren to dwell together in unity!"[10] Those "good and pleasant" times became more and more frequent toward the end of our third year. We actually began to enjoy one another! God had honored our heart attitudes and prayers, our communication and our commitment to working things through. In our minds, He had performed a miracle. We grew to miss each other when we were apart rather than being glad for the relief from pressure.

The summer of our third year together Jean returned from her family home in Houston and exclaimed, "Ney, do you remember my once mentioning someone named Doug? I knew him four years ago—and didn't like him very much."

"Yes," I said, "I recall your telling me about him."

"Well, when I was home, I saw him, and he asked me out to dinner. After dinner we drove to Galveston, sat on the beach one balmy evening, and visited for a long time. He's really changed since I knew him before. I really enjoyed being with him, which surprised me!"

Two months later Doug phoned Jean from Illinois to say he was coming to Dallas for a conference. They attended the conference together every day. When meetings weren't scheduled, they would visit, shop, or go sightseeing.

When Doug left to go home, Jean said, "Ney, I feel like a part of me is gone." The next thing I knew, they were writing back and forth, then phoning back and forth, then flying back and forth. I wasn't surprised when they became engaged in November.

One evening I received an unexpected phone call from Doug. "Ney, Jean and I have been talking, and I want you to know that we realize we could not be getting married apart from the things you two learned and worked through in your three years together. I want to thank you personally for your invest-ment in Jean's life."

The call touched me deeply, and I cried grateful, happy tears that night for all that God had done. The month before Jean left to be married, I could not mention her name without tears com-ing to my eyes. We had shared so much in those years, and I knew I would miss her deeply.

I had come to see that the sensitivity I had originally thought lacking in Jean's life had been there all the time. In fact, I marveled at the depth of her compassion and love. But it took all we experienced to bring it out.

Years later Jean wrote me, saying, "The experiences we had together have everything to do with my having a happy marriage. As you continued to love me, the walls of fear and hostility gradually began to crumble! After I learned to accept my own feelings of failure, fear, and depression, I could be patient and understanding of Doug's feelings too.

"Dating," she continued, "could not have prepared me for marriage. I was too guarded about my true feelings. I needed to live with someone who would confront me with the truth about myself and about herself."

I've often thought that it's much easier to love God than to love people. After all, He's perfect and we're not! That must account for Jesus' statement that the world would know that He is God by our love for one another. It is not natural, but supernatural, for us to love others with the kind of love and commitment that stays in there when feelings are saying, "I don't feel loving toward this person. I want out!" But Jean and I took God at His word: We chose to stay in relationship even when we both felt like getting out.

God used our relationship to teach both of us many things, particularly about what He means when He calls Christians to unity and forgiveness. It has nothing to do with our feelings and everything to do with God's sovereignty! During my years with Jean, I learned that to reject an office mate, roommate, husband, or wife is to reject God's provision, because God sovereignly places people together. Although in many ways Jean and I were opposites, the Lord brought us together in oneness and harmony. The love, commitment, gratefulness, and devotion we have in our hearts toward one another is powerful to this day.

CHAPTER 7

UNMASKING
THE ENEMY

When Jean and I first met Jackie Hudson, she was working in an office in Dallas, Texas, helping with preparations for EXPLO '72, a conference which would eventually draw over eighty thousand Christians to be trained in principles of evangelism and discipleship. Jackie was just entering Christian work and wanted with all her heart to serve and follow God. She was vivacious and outgoing, the picture of happiness.

When I saw her three months later, I couldn't believe the contrast. I was leaving a class to have lunch with a friend when I happened to see Jackie in the back of the room. She seemed off in another world. As I walked up to her, I noticed dark circles under her eyes; she looked very pale. I wondered if she was well.

"Jackie, you look awful." I was surprised at my own bluntness. "Are you okay?"

"No." Her lip began to quiver, and she was on the verge of tears.

I reached out to touch her shoulder. "Do you have a few minutes to talk?"

Jackie nodded, and tears began to run down her cheeks.

We moved outside to a grassy area on the campus and sat down. "Can you tell me what's wrong?" I asked.

She began, "Well, Ney, this may sound strange, but last month during EXPLO, when I was sitting in the Cotton Bowl, looking out at those eighty thousand people, some troubling thoughts flashed into my mind. Thoughts like, 'How do I really know there is a God? How do I know all these people aren't just fooling themselves?'"

She paused and took a deep breath. "I dismissed the doubts, but in the days that followed, they kept coming back. The more I questioned, the greater my doubts became. Now it's to the point that I don't know for sure about anything."

Jackie shifted positions on the grass, looked down, and then looked back at me. "One part of me knows that Christianity is real, but my doubts keep plaguing me, and I feel as if I can't believe."

The pitch in her voice raised. "My doubts seem true, and now I'm not even sure I'm a Christian. I haven't been able to sleep or eat. I've lost nine pounds. Sometimes I wonder if Satan has a hand in all this. I can't believe, but I want to… I can't…" Her voice cracked, and she began to sob. "I want to. But I feel as if I'm fooling myself."

Together we turned to some Scripture passages on faith and began to talk through them. I asked, "What is faith, Jackie?"

"I guess on the basis of what you've said, it's 'taking God at His word.' But, Ney, I don't even know if there is a God, so how can I take Him at His word?"

I told Jackie that there was a spiritual battle going on and that Satan had blinded her mind to the truths of Scripture. I asked her if I could pray for her. She said yes, and I prayed that she would be delivered from Satan's power, that God would give her grace to believe Him again. Before I left, I gave her a packet of Bible verses and encouraged her to spend time reading them and reflecting on them. We agreed to stay in touch.

The next day Jackie located me at a friend's home.

"Ney, since I saw you yesterday, I still haven't been able to sleep or eat. I don't know what to do."

"Do you have a Bible close by?" I asked.

"Yes."

"Okay. Turn to 1 Peter. I know you say you don't know if the Bible is true right now, but for a few minutes, let's just pretend you believe it is." I asked her to start reading aloud verses 6 through 10 of chapter 5.

She began, "Humble yourselves, therefore, under the mighty hand of God, that He may exalt you at the proper time."

"What does that tell you to do?" I asked.

"Humble myself."

"How do you humble yourself?"

She continued to read. "Casting all your anxiety upon Him, because He cares for you."

"How many anxieties?"

"All."

"And why are you supposed to do that?"

Jackie's voice sounded almost hopeful. "Because He cares for me."

"Yes," I answered. "He cares for you. Now read the next line."

"Be of sober spirit, be on the alert. Your adversary, the devil, prowls about like a roaring lion, seeking someone to devour."

"Now, Jackie, what is God's warning to you?"

"To be on the alert."

"Why?"

"Because the devil is out to get me."

"Who is the devil?"

"He is my adversary."

"Okay. Read the next verse."

"But resist him, firm in your faith, knowing that the same experiences of suffering are being accomplished by your brethren who are in the world."

"What does God tell you to do, Jackie?"

"Resist Satan."

"How are you to resist him?"

"By being firm in my faith."

"What is faith?"

"Taking God at His word."

"And what does the passage say next?"

"Knowing that the same experiences of suffering are being accomplished by your brethren who are in the world."

"Jackie, this means that you aren't alone in this! Other people are going through the same things you are. One of Satan's tricks is to make you think you are all alone.

"In the next verse, God promises, 'And after you have suffered for a little while, the God of all grace, who called you to His eternal glory in Christ, will Himself perfect, confirm, strengthen and establish you.' What you are going through won't last forever."

I continued. "I want you to memorize these verses. And since the whole passage talks about choosing to believe God's truth over

Satan's lies, I want you to write in the margin of your Bible these words: 'Choose to believe.'"

We said good-bye and arranged another time to meet.

A couple of days later we met in a restaurant. Again she said, "I desperately want to believe, but I can't."

"Jackie, you have built a pattern of believing the wrong things, and now you need to start building a pattern of believing the right things. You are thinking of yourself as not having faith, but you need to think, 'I am beginning to develop a new habit of walking by faith.'"

As Jackie and I continued to meet, I felt we made some progress, but I was still concerned for her. When she left for her staff assignment at Oregon State University, she was still very, very low.

In the days that followed, I continued to pray for her. A mutual friend gave me periodic updates on how Jackie was doing spiritually.

When I saw Jackie a year later, she was the picture of victory again. She told me some of the things she had learned. "The thing that freed me was realizing I was in a spiritual battle. I began to realize I had an old nature that was hostile toward God and prone to doubt. But I also had a new nature that could respond to God.

"I realized, too, that my will was the key. With my will I could choose to believe God and choose to take Him at His word, regardless of what my feelings or my old nature told me. When I began to get into the habit of believing God, my doubts faded."

The change came when Jackie chose to believe God's Word in the heat of a spiritual battle for her mind and will. She put her trust in God's promise that "greater is He who is in you than he who is in the world."[1]

Today Jackie has a positive, powerful ministry of helping people—especially those who have painful backgrounds. She has chronicled part of her journey in a book entitled *Doubt: A Road to Growth*.[2]

If I had met Jackie just a year earlier, I wouldn't have known what to say to her in the face of her doubts, because at that time I greatly underestimated the power and scope of Satan's influence. C. S. Lewis wrote that if Satan can get us to disbelieve his existence, he has won a major battle because his activity goes unrecognized. Though I believed in Satan's existence, I often acted as though I didn't. I didn't even like to talk about him; it seemed unnecessary and almost distasteful. But all that changed during the summer I moved to Dallas from Arrowhead Springs.

One day I was in my bedroom, talking aloud to the Lord, and I asked Him "to teach me to pray." As I spoke the words, I realized the phrase had a familiar ring to it. Long ago the disciples had asked the same thing of Jesus. I turned to the Lord's Prayer, which was Christ's answer to the disciples' request.

A phrase in the prayer, "And do not lead us into temptation, but deliver us from evil" stood out like a neon sign.[3] I recalled another of Christ's prayers, found in John 17, where Jesus prayed to the Father on behalf of believers who would remain on earth after He ascended to heaven, saying, "I do not ask You to take them out of the world, but to keep them from the evil one."[4]

I thought, *It's interesting that these two prayers of Jesus have one thing in common—a request to be delivered or kept from the Evil*

One, Satan. I began to pray almost daily that I would be kept from Satan's power. I knew I was praying in agreement with Jesus Christ, who would be interceding for me in heaven for the same thing.

As I began to learn more about Satan and his ways, I asked God to teach me what I should know about spiritual warfare. He led me to Ephesians 6.

> Finally, be strong in the Lord, and in the strength of His
> might. Put on the full armor of God, that you may be able to
> stand firm against the schemes of the devil. For our struggle is
> not against flesh and blood, but against the rulers, against the
> powers, against the world forces of this darkness, against the
> spiritual forces of wickedness in the heavenly places.
> Therefore, take up the full armor of God, that you may be
> able to resist in the evil day, and having done everything, to
> stand firm. Stand firm therefore, having girded your loins
> with truth, and having put on the breastplate of righteous-
> ness, and having shod your feet with the preparation of the
> gospel of peace; in addition to all, taking up the shield of faith
> with which you will be able to extinguish all the flaming mis-
> siles of the evil one.[5]

This passage reveals many things about Satan, and among the most important is that he is a deceiver. He makes something seem like the truth when it is not. Good magicians, for example, have mastered the art of deception. This passage exposes Satan as a deceptive schemer—wily, crafty, and deceitful. Jesus called him the "father of lies."[6] Satan's schemes take many forms, and his strategies are infinite in their variety. At times he will make an all-out attack; at other times he is subtle. But Paul also writes that we can counter Satan's attacks with the shield of faith. We can actually extinguish all of Satan's flaming missiles, or "fiery darts," as the *King James Version* puts it.

What are these "fiery darts"? And how can we "take up the shield of faith" to extinguish them? Just as in a war the enemy has an advantage if he is camouflaged, so Satan has a particular advantage over us if his tactics aren't disclosed.

Doubt is one of Satan's most effective fiery darts. He has used this weapon to keep thousands of Christians living lives of defeat and despair, just as he had Jackie. They struggle because they have stopped believing God and are choosing to believe their doubt-filled thoughts rather than the Word of God.

In the Garden of Eden Satan approached Eve with the taunting words, "Indeed, has God said…?"[7] Satan wanted to undermine Eve's trust, confidence, and belief in God and His word. He does the same thing today. And he wins every time, unless his victim chooses to believe God, just as Jackie did.

Scripture refers to Satan as "the accuser of our brethren,"[8] and *condemnation* is another one of his fiery darts. At times when I have felt condemned for no apparent reason, I've turned to Romans 8 in response to Satan's attacks.

> There *is* therefore *now no* condemnation for those who are in Christ Jesus…. If God is for us, who is against us? He who did not spare His own Son, but delivered Him up for us all, how will He not also with Him freely give us all things? Who will bring a charge against God's elect? God is the one who

justifies; who is the one who condemns? Christ Jesus is He who died, yes, rather who was raised, who is at the right hand of God, who also intercedes for us.[9]

When I feel condemnation, I read this passage and then pray, "Lord, I feel condemned, but I choose to believe what Your Word says. Thank You that I am not condemned by You." I've found the simple affirmation of the truth of God's Word to be my most effective counterattack.

Satan's third tactic is to tempt us with the feeling that *God has forsaken us.* I've had times in my life when I've felt very lost and alone, as if no one cared about what I was going through and even God was oblivious to me. This feeling often arose out of an emotionally trying situation and was a natural initial response.

But Satan's tactic has been to take that feeling one step further—until I've actually begun believing that not only does no one care about me, but that God Himself has withdrawn His love and concern to the point of completely giving up on me.

Sometimes this feeling leads people to desperate, even suicidal, thoughts. When I find my mind veering in that direction, I like to listen to these encouraging words from Romans 8:

Who shall separate us from the love of Christ? Shall tribulation, or distress, or persecution, or famine, or nakedness, or peril, or sword?... But in all these things we overwhelmingly conquer through Him who loved us. For I am convinced that neither death, nor life, nor angels, nor principalities, nor things present, nor things to come, nor powers, nor height, nor depth, nor any other created thing, shall be able to separate us from the love of God, which is in Christ Jesus our Lord.[10]

Paul is saying that nothing can separate us from the love of God. In fact, God Himself promised, "I will never desert you, nor will I ever forsake you."[11] The word *never* does not convey the force of His statement. In the original language the word used is called a "triple negative," and there is no single-word English equivalent. In essence, He was saying, *"I will never, no never, no never leave you or forsake you."*

A fiery dart that is closely related to thoughts of being forsaken by God is *a sense of worthlessness.* I once heard someone say that infants still in their mother's arms are constantly receiving love and positive attention. They are told, "I love you, you precious little baby." But as they grow up, various experiences of rejection—from their families or the outside world—may take their toll and completely negate all the positive input they received as children. As a result, by the time they reach adulthood, they may feel worthless.

In fact, Satan uses anything and everything he can to undermine our sense of personal worth. He attacks our feelings in order to sabotage our faith. He hates us, and if he can get us to hate ourselves and doubt our value, especially to God, then he has successfully convinced us to think exactly the opposite of what God tells us in His Word.

Sometimes he shoots a fiery dart of worthlessness toward us just after we have sinned. God loves who we are, although He doesn't always love what we do. He deals with us to correct our *behavior,* whereas Satan wants to destroy our person, our *character.*

For example, let's suppose you tell a lie. Satan might say, "You liar! You're nothing but a liar, and you know it. You'll never be worth anything."

In contrast, God says, "I love you, but you did not tell the truth. I love you too much to let you continue doing that, so we need to correct that behavior."

God loves us. We are "precious" in His sight![12] In fact, as mind-boggling as it may be and as hard as it is to comprehend, we are worth as much to God as His own Son is. He gave His Son for us. If we are worth that much to God, it can only be the Adversary himself who tries to make us feel worthless.

When Satan has attacked me in this way, I have prayed, "Lord, I feel worthless. But I thank You that I am worth as much to You as Your own dear Son."

When Satan directs his assaults at us individually, those efforts are but a tiny part of his ultimate strategy for crippling the entire body of Christ. And sometimes, without our realizing it, he employs us to do his work for him. How? Through *criticism,* which destroys unity among believers. Since Jesus prayed that His followers be "one," we know that any discord among us cannot be from God but from the Evil One.

Those of us who have been hurt by words that others have spoken behind our backs know how painful criticism can be. That pain can motivate us to keep from speaking hurtful words about anyone else. That's what helped Jean and me to keep our commitment to give good reports about one another to other people. At times we sought counsel from others about our relationship but only when we had agreed to do so.

In his book *My Utmost for His Highest,* Oswald Chambers teaches that discernment is for the purpose of prayer and not for finding fault.[13] Because none of us is perfect, we inevitably see things in other people's lives that we don't like or with which we don't agree. Some of these observations may be valid; however, when we become negative and judgmental about those things, the result can be momentary spiritual defeat, leading to frustration and worry. On the other hand, if we take the things about others that are hard to accept and prayerfully give them to God, we are working in cooperation with God, not Satan. We are acknowledging His ability to do what He wants in lives and in difficult situations.

That brings us to the dart in Satan's arsenal that I like to call the "fiery dart of *if only.*" Satan used this dart on Eve in order to persuade her to disobey God and eat of the tree of the knowledge of good and evil.[14] In essence he said, "Eve, this tree limits you. If only it weren't for this tree, you would know everything God knows."

To this day, Satan tries to convince us that we are limited, first by one thing and then another. He speaks in subtle ways, saying, "This person—your wife, husband, child, roommate, office mate, relative, parent—limits you. If only he or she weren't in your life, things would almost be perfect."

When Jean and I lived together, Satan would whisper, "Ney, Jean limits you. If it weren't for her, you would be a lot happier, and life would be much better for you." Had I believed Satan, I would have begun acting on my belief and would have lived for the day when Jean and I would no longer be roommates.

But I knew I needed to look past my feelings about our situation and put my hope in God and His Word. As my friend Don Meredith has said, "We need to see the people around us as no limitation to us."

The Old Testament tells the story of Joseph, who was hated by his brothers. They threw him into a pit and sold him into slavery. From all outward appearances, his circumstances limited Joseph. He could have thought, *If only my brothers hadn't done this, I'd be free!* Instead, Joseph chose to hope in the Lord, who brought good out of the evil Joseph's brothers had done. Years later Joseph told his brothers, "You intended to harm me, but God intended it for good to accomplish what is now being done, the saving of many lives."[15]

After their brother Lazarus had been dead for four days, Mary and Martha each came to Jesus and said, "Lord, if You had been here, my brother would not have died."[16] Jesus met their "if" with His "if." He responded, "Did I not say to you, *if you believe, you will see the glory of God?*"[17] Moments later He raised Lazarus from the dead.

We must believe God for the "if onlys" in our lives, for the people or the circumstances that we feel are limiting us. He is able to bring glory out of all those things.

Doubt, condemnation, feeling forsaken or worthless, criticism, thoughts of "if only"—these are just a sampling of the sinister, devious feelings and strategies the Evil One uses to attack our faith in God and His Word. Satan truly "prowls about like a roaring lion." He seeks to devour us all, and he often does it by hurling one fiery dart at a time. The cumulative effect of his attacks can immobilize anyone who does not take up the shield of faith against him.

Such was the case with someone whom I met a few years ago.

I had flown to the East Coast to spend time with some staff women there. Barbie Leyden met me at the airport, saying, "Ney, I am very concerned about Marti. She's just not herself anymore.

She is very depressed and seems to have given up on life. Would you spend some time with her?"

The first time we met I could tell almost instantaneously that Marti's will had become completely passive. She told me that a particular young man had fallen in love with her and that she had responded wholeheartedly. She prayed, asking God whether they were to be married, and she told me that she felt God had spoken to her from certain scriptures and confirmed that they would marry. She had claimed those Bible verses, believing they supported her hopes.

But the relationship didn't develop as she had hoped. As a result, she lost all faith and confidence in God. She just didn't care anymore. She refused to take to heart anything I said, and as we talked further, she became a "slippery fish," making evasive statements.

When I left our appointment, I realized I hadn't been able to get through to Marti in any way. Heavily burdened, I began to pray fervently about our next time together. I remembered these words from 2 Timothy: "With gentleness correcting those who are in opposition, if perhaps God may grant them repentance leading to the knowledge of the truth, and they may come to their senses and escape from the snare of the devil, having been held captive by him to do his will."[18] These verses seemed to speak to this situation.

I said, "Father, I pray You will grant Marti repentance leading to the knowledge of the truth, and I pray she will come to her senses and escape from the snare of the devil, having been held captive by him to do his will. Father, I pray that she will give her will back to You and that there will be new light and new hope and a new beginning for her."

The next day we met again. I told her I had been thinking about her since we last talked. "When you prayed that you would marry this fellow," I said, "and claimed verses to that effect, and it didn't happen, you lost confidence in God and His Word, right?"

"That's right," she responded. "I believe God let me down."

"You know, Marti, nowhere in the Bible does it say 'so-and-so will be your husband.' God didn't let you down. You wanted the Bible to say that, and you read that into some verses, didn't you?"

She agreed.

"Rather than losing confidence in God and His Word, you need to lose confidence in your reading *into* His Word something that it doesn't say." She thought for a moment, and then said she hadn't looked at it that way.

Then I told her how dangerous it was for her will to be in a passive state. I said, "Marti, I'd like to hear you say, 'I want to be out of this.'" But once again she seemed to slip away, and she began to speak vaguely and evasively.

I shared with her the passage from 2 Timothy. As I read the verses, she seemed to hear me for the first time as she grasped a sense of the importance of what was happening. She told me, "I thought God was going to do everything to get me out of this, but I see now that my will needs to be active. I thought God was responsible to get me out of my depressions and downhill trends, but I never knew I had a part until today."

I told her that her part was to take her "mustard seed" of faith[19] and choose to believe God's Word. Because all of her thoughts were despairing and led her to question God, I suggested that she begin keeping a daily journal. I encouraged her to write out all of her negative, doubtful thoughts and then to end her thought progression with something from God's Word that would speak directly to the feelings she had just expressed. For instance, if her thoughts led her to believe that God had forsaken her, she should end the journal page with Jesus' words, "I will never desert you, nor will I ever forsake you."[20]

I told her I knew that, in the depths of her heart, she wanted to be out of her despondency but she needed to exercise her will. Then I suggested we pray together.

"I've prayed so many times, and it doesn't work," she said.

"But I want to enter into this with you," I responded, "and bear your burdens by praying with you. You have thought of yourself as having no faith and as not believing. I want you to think instead, *I'm beginning to develop a new habit of taking God at His word.* Give yourself time to develop this new habit. I'll commit myself to pray for you every day for the next two months."

So we prayed together. She told the Lord that she had given her will over to unbelief, but now she wanted to give her will to Him, to take Him at His word. I prayed for her and encouraged her to seek prayer support from others, since she hadn't told anyone else what she was going through.

Later that day I wrote in my journal, "I believe this could be a turning point in Marti's life. I pray that it will be."

Two days later I called her. She had just spent over three hours in Scripture and was beginning to see how she had been deceived in various ways. She said, "I believed that my life was going downhill, but 2 Corinthians 3:18 says we are being transformed 'from glory to glory.' Most of all, now I can see the part my will has to play in allowing God to change me."

Marti seemed grateful for my call, and I was pleased to see that she was beginning to form the habit of believing God.

Many years have passed since then. My friend not only came out of her despondency, but she has been serving the Lord successfully since that time. As both Jackie and Marti discovered, we must align our wills with the truth of Scripture, because Satan will keep sending flaming missiles and fiery darts to undermine our faith. He comes in many different forms, planting seeds of doubt and unbelief in our hearts and minds any way he can.

But we must also remember that he is a defeated foe. Christ won the battle over Satan on the cross, and as we remember our position in Christ, we can operate from that vantage point of victory.

The apostle Paul understood our victorious position. He wrote,

I pray that the eyes of your heart may be enlightened, so that you may know what is the hope of His calling, what are the riches of the glory of His inheritance in the saints, and what is the surpassing greatness of His power toward us who believe. These are in accordance with the working of the strength of His might which He brought about in Christ, when He raised Him from the dead, and seated Him at His right hand in the heavenly places, far above all rule and authority and power and dominion, and every name that is named, not only in this age, but also in the one to come. And He put all things in subjection under His feet, and gave Him as head over all things to the church, which is His body, the fulness of Him who fills all in all.[21]

As we walk through life and face various spiritual battles, we need to assume our rightful position in Christ, as clearly spelled out in His Word. Above all, we must take up the shield of faith with which we will be able to extinguish *all* the fiery darts of the Evil One.

CHAPTER 8

OBJECTIFYING
LIFE'S PAIN

Life's trials and struggles can cause us to feel greatly discouraged. My friend, Don Meredith, founder of Christian Family Life, a family counseling and teaching ministry, has an interesting theory about such times.

One day his secretary, Carol, was telling him about all the difficult circumstances she was facing. When she finished, Don said, "Carol, what you have just told me is not unusual. Seventy-five percent of life is made up of struggles, concerns, frustrations, and trials. That 75 percent will always be with you. You need to let that 75 percent be characterized not by unbelief but by faith, by believing God and hoping in Him."

Then he added whimsically, "And as for the remaining 25 percent, trust the Lord and go out and have a good time."

When Carol related the conversation to me, I thought Don's counsel contained great wisdom. Jesus Himself taught that in this world we would have troubles.[1] Yet we are often deceived into thinking we really shouldn't have problems and that "happiness is just around the corner."

We get caught up in the "when-then" syndrome:

When I'm out of school, then everything will be okay.
When I get married, then I'll be happy.
When I get out of this hard spot, then everything will be fine.

And on it goes.
But that's not what usually happens.

As Don suggested, we can expect to go through difficulties and heartaches in this life. We will feel pain, but we may not know how to respond in a way that promotes spiritual growth. Understandably, it is often hard to isolate these incidents, to stand back and evaluate what is going on. As a result, we may never benefit from the experience.

I have learned that a significant part of walking by faith every day is being objective about life's experiences. I use a simple chart—I call it my Objectifying Chart—to help me think through a difficult or challenging circumstance.

First, I divide a piece of paper into four parts or sections.

In the first section I record *every good* and *positive thing* I can think of about the situation. For example, if my struggles center around a certain person, I write down everything I like about that individual.

In the second section I list all the *negative aspects* I can think of about the matter; particularly those things that I dislike about the person or situation or that are hard for me to accept.

Someone has said that negative circumstances and people do not put negative reactions in our hearts; they merely reveal what is already there. The old adage "He brings out the worst in me" holds a good deal of truth. "He" didn't put in "the worst," but he did bring it out! Often I'm not aware of the negatives in my heart until something comes into my life to expose them.

In section three I write down my responses to the negative things I wrote in section two. I try to be honest about my inner reactions and feelings. In the process God always brings to light an attitude that needs to be confessed, such as hate, irritability, lack of forgiveness, or impatience. Then I confess to the Lord all the things I have written down. Often the attitudes listed are just the opposite of the fruit of the Spirit—love, joy, peace, patience, kindness, goodness, faithfulness, gentleness, and self-control.[2] I say, "Lord, I agree with You that I am wrong and You are right."

In section four I write down what God seems to want to teach me through my situation. For instance, if I find hate in my heart, then God might want to teach me how to love. If I find impatience, perhaps He wants to teach me patience. Then I pull out a good Bible concordance or a helpful guide such as *Nave's Topical Bible* to find appropriate verses to meet my need. (See page 102 for a sample chart.)

After I have put all my thoughts and feelings on paper, I go back and thank God for everything I've written in sections two and three. I do this, knowing that He will work even these things together for good in my life.

When I see my responses in the third section, although they fall far short of Scripture's teachings, I have learned not to get down on myself or become discouraged. I may grieve over the sin in my heart, but I do not condemn myself, because God doesn't condemn me.[3] Rather, I am free to admit my sinfulness, knowing that to be truthful with God about what is in my heart is the first step toward change.

1. THINGS I LIKE	2. THINGS I DON'T LIKE
3. MY REACTIONS OR MY RESPONSES	4. WHAT GOD MIGHT WANT TO TEACH ME, OR SCRIPTURES TO MEET MY NEED

The small but powerful book *The Practice of the Presence of God* by Brother Lawrence has encouraged me in this area. This seventeenth-century Christian walked closely with the Lord, and when he sinned, he would lift up his hand toward heaven and say to God, "I shall never do otherwise if You leave me to myself."[4] Brother Lawrence knew that he needed God's help and power to live the Christian life.

I have often prayed Brother Lawrence's words and then have added, "Father, do for me by Your Holy Spirit what I cannot do for myself."

I used to look at Scripture as a law or a threat that was being held over my head, condemning me for not living up to its standards. Now I see that God's Word is not meant to be a threat, but a promise of all that He wants to do in my life by His Spirit.

Through the years people have said to me, "Ney, I have confessed a particular sin over and over, but I still struggle in that area. I haven't seen any progress." Then they'll name a specific action or attitude that could be placed in section three of the chart.

I often respond by asking, "Are you renewing your mind with a portion of Scripture that speaks to the sin you have confessed?" More often than not, they will say they had not thought of doing that. For example, they may have confessed that they are impatient, but they have not gone on to gain God's perspective by meditating on a passage of Scripture that deals with patience.

Since God convicts us of specific sin in our lives, we need to confess those sins specifically. Then we need to fill our minds with a portion of God's Word that relates specifically to what we've confessed. Then the Holy Spirit can use that portion of Scripture to renew our minds with God's perspective.

Using this chart to objectify our experiences helps us take personal responsibility for our behavior and reactions. It also encourages us to find a passage of Scripture that addresses that behavior or reaction. In this way the person or circumstance that seemed to be a millstone around our neck becomes a blessing God uses to teach us about Himself or about what He wants to do in us.

One of those circumstances came into my life in January of 1977.

It all began when Robert Pittenger, then an assistant to Dr. Bright, greeted me as he arrived at my home for dinner. "Ney, I've been thinking that you should go to the presidential inauguration in Washington, D.C. Carol Lawrence has been asked by the president to sing, and since we will be hosting her while she's there, it would be nice if you could go and be with her."

The whole matter seemed fantastic but far-fetched to me.

"I really do appreciate your wanting me to go, Robert, but I don't know. God would have to do a lot to work out all the details on such short notice. I leave on a trip in a couple of days, so I'll just assume I'm not going unless I hear from you."

Two days later I flew to Seattle to speak at a staff conference, then on to Little Rock, Arkansas, for another meeting. I arrived in Little Rock in the late afternoon and checked into my hotel. There was a message awaiting me at the front desk, asking me to call Dr. Bright's office in Arrowhead Springs.

I dialed the number, and Jim Pratt, another assistant to Dr. Bright, answered. "Ney, Dr. Bright definitely wants you to go to the inauguration."

"He really does, Jim?"

"Yes, it's all set. They're expecting you."

I hung up the phone in a daze. I exclaimed aloud, "Is this really happening to me? Lord, what will I wear?" I had nothing that would be suitable for such a formal occasion, nor did I have enough money to buy anything.

During my introductory remarks that night, I told the conferees my news, adding that although I normally would stay for the entire conference, I would be leaving early to go to Dallas and then on to the inauguration. The conferees were excited for me.

I returned to my hotel room that evening, my mind filled with thoughts of concern and worry over what I would wear to the inauguration. I sat in bed, pillows propped up behind my back, and picked up my Bible. I started filling in the objectifying chart and began to analyze the situation carefully.

I liked the thought of going to Washington D.C. I didn't like not having the right clothes to wear or the money to buy them. My reaction was to become anxious. I hadn't been aware of some of the worry and unbelief in my heart until this incident revealed it. I confessed my anxiety, realizing that the Lord wanted to teach me faith.

Then I remembered a passage in the Sermon on the Mount in which Jesus spoke to those who were anxious about food and clothing. I quickly turned there and began to read:

> For this reason I say to you, do not be anxious for your life, as
> to what you shall eat, or what you shall drink; nor for your
> body, as to what you shall put on.... Observe how the lilies of
> the field grow; they do not toil nor do they spin, yet I say to

you that even Solomon in all his glory did not clothe himself like one of these. But if God so arrays the grass of the field, which is alive today and tomorrow is thrown into the furnace, will He not much more do so for you, O men [and women] of little faith?[5]

After I read this passage, I prayed, "Lord, I confess to You that I'm anxious about what I shall put on. But You say here that You clothe the lilies and the grass and that You'll do much more for me. I do confess my 'little faith.' I want to believe You!"

I continued to read:

Do not be anxious then, saying, "What shall we eat?" or "What shall we drink?" or "With what shall we clothe ourselves?" For all these things the Gentiles eagerly seek; for your heavenly Father knows that you need all these things. But seek first His kingdom and His righteousness; and all these things shall be added to you.[6]

Once again I prayed: "Oh, Lord, as best I know how, I am seeking first Your kingdom and Your righteousness. But I'm so glad that You know my needs, that You will take care of me, and that all these things 'will be added' to me. I believe Your Word is truer than how I feel right now, and I pray that You will provide—and I thank You for how You will do that."

Here—on page 107—is what I wrote down on my objectifying chart:

1. THINGS I LIKE	2. THINGS I DON'T LIKE
Opportunity to go to DC *Opportunity to go to the inauguration*	*Not having the right clothes to wear* *No money to buy clothes*

3. MY REACTIONS OR MY RESPONSES	4. WHAT GOD MIGHT WANT TO TEACH ME, OR SCRIPTURES TO MEET MY NEED
anxious *worried* *unbelief that God can meet my needs*	*Matt. 6:25,28-30* *Matt. 6:31-33* *Trust in Him to provide. If He clothed the lilies, He can clothe me.* *Believe He will take care of me.* *Seek first His kingdom, and He will add to me what I need.*

I turned off the lights and slipped under the covers. I lay there drifting into sleep, singing the little song, "Seek and ye shall find, knock and the door shall be opened…" It occurred to me I could start "seeking" and "knocking" by looking for some clothes to borrow.

The next morning I realized I needed to cash a small check to cover the rest of my trip. My friend, Carol Wierman, was registrar for the conference and offered to cash the check for me.

She brought me the money while I was sitting in the back of a room during a meeting. Kneeling by my chair, she handed me two extra $10 bills and whispered, "Ney, I'd like this to go toward something for your trip."

I handed the extra money back to her. "Carol," I protested, "you're dear to do this, but I can't take it!"

She handed the bills back insistently. "Ney, I want you to have it. I believe the Lord wants me to give it to you." Carol walked away, leaving me with a lump in my throat and two $10 bills in my lap.

Later in the day, another friend at the conference, Ann Parkinson, handed me a note. My mouth fell open when I unfolded it and out fell $30. I was still holding the note when Don Meredith, the conference speaker, came up to me and said, "Well, have you been shopping yet for the inauguration?"

"No, Don, I really wasn't planning on shopping. I thought I'd borrow something to wear."

He was indignant. "I don't want you to borrow anything. I want you to buy yourself a new outfit. Can we give you $150?" Before I could answer, he had his checkbook out. I was speechless!

Late that night I sat in my hotel room, my chin resting in my hands, staring at three $10 bills, one $20 bill, and a check for $150. I worshiped the Lord as I viewed the money that I'd received in direct response to my need less than twenty-four hours after my prayer. I was overwhelmed with joy.

I called a friend long-distance to share with her my elation over what the Lord had done. After I related the story, she said, "I'd like to add $25 to what the Lord has already given."

And there was still more to come.

I left Little Rock on Sunday and decided to stop in Dallas. My good friend Mary Graham and I had been invited to a church building dedication that evening. I met Mary at the airport, and as we arrived at the church, Ann West, another friend of mine, rushed up to us.

"Ney, what are you doing in Dallas?"

"Annie, you won't believe this, but I'm on my way to the inauguration."

"Really? That's great! What are you going to wear?"

"Funny you should ask. I plan to shop for something tomorrow. And Ann Parkinson suggested I call a friend of hers to borrow a couple of long dresses."

"You don't need to do that! I have some things I know you could wear. Come on over tonight."

Midnight found me going through Ann's closet, trying on black velvet skirts and lovely gowns. When Mary and I left the Wests' home a little later, I had two elegant gowns that would be suitable for any evening event in Washington.

The next day, with the money I'd been given at the Little Rock conference, I bought a beautiful five-piece suit with skirt and slacks at an exclusive Dallas department store. The woman doing my alterations was hemming the slacks when I remarked, "You know, this is the most expensive outfit I've ever bought."

"Ya gotta be kiddin'!" she said in a strong New York accent, looking up in surprise.

"No, it really is."

"Well, what's the deal?" she asked. "Where are you going?"

"Do you really want to know?"

"Yeah, tell me."

I told her about my invitation to the inauguration, how I didn't have anything to wear, and how God had provided for my needs miraculously. With reverence in her voice she said, "I've been head of this department for seven years. I've never done this before, and I will never do it again, but because you've told me this story, I'm not going to charge you anything for the alteration." Not only did she make the alterations free of charge, but she completed in two hours what often takes several days.

That night as I was packing to leave for Washington, I surveyed my clothing: two lovely gowns, a new suit, a new purse, shoes, and some new costume jewelry. The Lord had done "exceeding abundantly" beyond all that I could have asked or thought.[7]

The next morning Mary bade me good-bye at the Dallas airport. As I waited to board my plane, I felt a little anxious about the new and different situations I would be facing over the next few days. I pulled out my Bible and turned to Matthew 6. The chapter's last verse stood out: "Therefore do not be anxious for tomorrow; for tomorrow will care for itself. Each day has enough trouble of its own."[8]

I silently prayed, "Lord, I thank You again for Your miraculous provision for me. Thank You for the opportunity to go to Washington. Now I choose to believe that tomorrow will care for itself and that You will take care of me. I don't have grace yet for my tomorrows, but I thank You that Your grace will be sufficient when tomorrow comes."

The announcement came to board the plane. I boarded and sat next to a distinguished couple who also happened to be going to the inauguration. The husband had many titles, including the former head of the Bureau of Indian Affairs. By the time we landed, they had invited me to be their guest at the American Indian Inaugural Ball!

Robert, who had first mentioned to me the possibility of attending the inauguration, was at the Washington National Airport to meet my plane. "Ney, Carol Lawrence's agent just called to say she is ill and won't be able to come."

"That's okay. I'm sorry to hear Carol is sick, but the Lord has already outdone Himself for me. I know I'm here for a purpose."

The Lord's blessing on my trip was evident in countless ways. I made many new friends, visited the White House and Executive Office Building, attended the American Indian Ball, and observed the nation's capital in festive transition.

And I had some important spiritual lessons reinforced during those exciting days of preparation. I believe the turnabout in my attitude concerning the inauguration came when I recognized my anxiety and made it a point to get into a portion of Scripture that would speak to my need.

I was anxious and needed clothes. I could have dwelt on my feelings and kept worrying, which I have done in the past. But, with the help of my Objectifying Chart, I went on to gain God's perspective on the situation. By reading Matthew 6, I was able to renew my mind with God's words and see my situation from His perspective. I was honest with Him about my feelings, but I chose to believe Scripture instead of how I felt. Long before I felt that my need would be met, I claimed His promises that He would meet my need.

The crises in our lives come in varying degrees, from small difficulties to major conflicts. Whether we're faced with the normal ups and downs of life or the most devastating circumstances we've ever encountered, we need to remember that life's difficulties can turn out to be God's greatest supernatural blessings for us—if we are willing to objectify our experiences and trust Him in the midst of them.

CHAPTER 9

FAILURE AND
THE PHANTOM

At times my relationship with God has been so close and satisfying that I've thought, *For the rest of my life, all I will do is just love and serve and please Him. I'm finally getting the picture of the Christian life, finally walking in victory. From now on, everything will be just fine.*

But just about the time I think I've got it all together and that I'll never fail again, I surprise myself. I fail. And because I'm surprised, I assume that God is surprised too.

One time after I had failed, I became terribly depressed and despondent. I wondered how someone as sinful as I ever wound up in Christian work. Jean and I were living together at the time, and she noticed my despondency. She said sympathetically, "Ney, God is not surprised that you failed."

Hardly believing her words, I exclaimed, "He's not?"

As if to reinforce the truth for my heart, Jean repeated, "No, God is not surprised that you failed."

"But sometimes I wish I could just be perfect. I don't want to sin, but I always fall short of my standard of perfection. I am very discouraged by my failure."

"I understand how you feel, Ney. You know, it's interesting, but at the point in time when we accept Christ, we know that we are totally loved and forgiven. But as we grow in the Christian life, something happens.

"Maybe we begin comparing ourselves with other people who seem more spiritually mature, or we look at the standards of an organization to which we belong, or we look at the standards of Scripture. When we fall short of any of those standards, we start condemning ourselves. When that happens, we have forgotten that God is the one who causes the growth and gives the increase.[1]

"So no matter where we are right now in our growth, we are right on schedule. We are still totally loved and accepted by Him. God is not surprised that we are where we are."

I listened with great interest as she continued. "What can happen is that a great gap forms between where we want to be and where we actually are, between the phantom image in our minds of where we think we should be spiritually and where we are in reality. So we start trying to bridge the gap in our own strength.

"Then we start trying to perform in the flesh, to grow spiritually by self-effort, forgetting that as we seek the Lord and His ways, His Spirit is the One who causes the growth in us."

I had tended to think that God accepted me when I was being obedient, when all was going well in my Christian life. But I couldn't see how God could love and accept me when I stumbled and failed, when I was falling flat on my face spiritually and life was looking dark and difficult because of my mistakes.

As Jean talked, I began to sense relief from internal pressure for the first time in several days. She was making a lot of sense as she shared God's perspective. I was beginning to see that even though I had failed, He hadn't given up on me.

She reminded me that God loved and accepted me regardless of my performance—a reminder that encouraged me to want my life to come in line with His Word in every way. And even though *forgiveness* means that a debt is canceled as if it never happened, the awareness that God had forgiven me did not make me think I was being given a license to sin willfully and go my own way. Instead, His love motivated me to want to please Him in every area of my life.

I realized that I could not look inside myself and find peace or look at my merits or performance and find justification. But I could look at what God said about me—my forgiveness and my position and acceptance in Christ—and choose with my will to believe His Words of truth and find peace.

Paul wrote, "Therefore having been justified by faith, we have peace with God through our Lord Jesus Christ."[2] While my position in Christ remained unchanging, my daily condition—my behavior and performance—was variable and changing.

God does not put His children on probation. Even before He showered His love, mercy, and grace on us, He knew our weaknesses and frailties. He knows that we are not Christians who became human beings at a point in time; rather, we are human beings who became Christians at a point in time.

Since Christ died for me while I was a helpless, ungodly, sinful enemy, I can do nothing to improve my image and make Him love me more. He loved me as much then as He ever had and as much as He ever will.[3] Jesus said, "Just as the Father has loved Me, I have also loved you."[4] Just as God will not take back His love from Jesus, neither will He take back His love from me. He made an eternal covenant with me that will never be broken.

How do I know that God will look at me and my failures with understanding, mercy, and forgiveness? One way I know is through the example of Jesus.

Forgiveness and compassion characterized Christ's earthly ministry. He freed the adulteress from her sin in the presence of those ready to stone her. As He hung on the cross, He forgave those who had crucified Him, and He gave eternal life to the criminal being crucified with Him. Jesus visibly demonstrated the forgiveness of God.

But of the numerous instances in which Jesus forgave people, I'm most encouraged by how He treated Peter after he had failed. Simon Peter was one of the first disciples to follow Jesus. Peter often acted with spontaneity and wholeheartedness. He was giving, thoughtful, loyal, and protective of Christ. He demonstrated great faith, spoke the truth from his heart, and said what he thought. Peter was one of Christ's closest friends while He was on the earth. Peter loved Jesus with abandon.

But Peter's devotion to Christ was never more evident than at the Last Supper. As Jesus gathered His disciples around Him to tell them what the next hours and days would hold, He turned His attention to Peter.

> "Simon, Simon, behold, Satan has demanded permission to sift you like wheat; but I have prayed for you, that your faith may not fail; and you, when once you have turned again, strengthen your brothers." And he said to Him, "Lord, with You I am ready to go both to prison and to death!" And He

said, "I say to you, Peter, the cock will not crow today until you have denied three times that you know Me."…

Peter said to Him, "Even if I have to die with You, I will not deny You."[5]

Peter couldn't imagine ever denying that he knew Jesus, and even when Christ told him of the imminent denial, Peter refused to believe he could ever do such a thing.

And then came the moment that Peter could not conceive of ever happening. The hours following the Last Supper had been traumatic and painful. Peter had gone with Christ to the Garden of Gethsemane, where he had witnessed Judas betraying Jesus. Peter, upset over the betrayal and Christ's abusive arrest by Roman officials, impulsively drew a sword and cut off the ear of the high priest's slave.

Luke records the events following Jesus' arrest:

And having arrested Him, they led Him away, and brought Him to the house of the high priest; but Peter was *following at a distance*. And after they had kindled a fire in the middle of the courtyard and had sat down together, Peter was sitting among them. And a certain servant-girl, seeing him as he sat in the firelight, and looking intently at him, said, "This man was with Him too." But he denied it, saying, "Woman, I do not know Him." And a little later, another saw him and said, "You are one of them too!" But Peter said, "Man, I am not!" And after about an hour had passed, another man began to insist, saying, "Certainly this man also was with Him, for he is a Galilean too." But Peter said, "Man, I do not know what you are talking about." And immediately, while he was still speaking, a cock crowed. And the Lord *turned and looked* at Peter. And Peter *remembered the word of the Lord,* how He had told him, "Before a cock crows today, you will deny Me three times." And he went out and *wept bitterly.*[6]

Jesus was not surprised when Peter failed. He had even prayed earlier that this disciple's faith would not fail. (Notice that Jesus' prayer wasn't that Peter wouldn't fail but that Peter's *faith* wouldn't fail.)

When Christ told Peter that He had prayed that his faith wouldn't fail, I believe He wanted Peter to believe that He would still love him and forgive him, even if he failed. In essence, Jesus was telling him, "In spite of what happens, Peter, I want you to believe what I have told you. I want you to take Me at My word that I love you...that you have forgiveness."

Further evidence that Christ had forgiven Peter came on Resurrection morning. Mary Magdalene and two other grieving followers of Jesus had just discovered the empty tomb—empty, that is, except for an angel sitting in the tomb, waiting to give them the message that the Savior was risen.

I've always loved what the angel said: "He has risen; He is not here; behold, here is the place where they laid Him. *But go, tell his disciples and Peter.*"[7] Here the Lord shows a special concern for Peter's state of mind. When Peter heard the news of the Resurrection, he literally ran to the tomb to see for himself that Jesus had risen.

Christ made a number of post-Resurrection appearances during the forty days before His ascension. One of those appearances sheds even more light on His forgiveness of Peter.

One day Peter and the other disciples went fishing on the Sea of Galilee and had little success. They fished through the night and caught nothing.

As the next day was breaking, Jesus appeared on the beach and called out to them, "Children, you do not have any fish, do you?"

The disciples, who had not yet recognized who He was, answered, "No." Then Jesus instructed them, "Cast the net on the right-hand side of the boat, and you will find a catch."

The disciples cast the net and caught so many fish that the men, several of whom were fishermen by trade, couldn't haul in the net. When this happened, John said to Peter, "It is the Lord." And when Peter heard those words, he threw himself into the sea, swimming as fast as he could to reach Jesus on shore.[8]

If Peter hadn't known that he was forgiven for his failure and that he was still loved by the Lord, would he have jumped from the boat out of eagerness to see Jesus? More than likely, he would have covered himself with the nets and hidden in the bottom of the boat. Then when the disciples came to shore and Jesus asked, "Where's Peter?" they would have answered, "Lord, he is afraid of You. He doesn't want to see You because he knows how angry You'll be with him for what he did."

But Peter was so convinced of Jesus' love and forgiveness that as soon as he realized it was Jesus on the shore, he swam the length of a football field to meet Him.

Peter had been with the Lord day and night for at least three years. He had heard Christ teach on forgiveness; he had seen Him forgive others. He may have even heard Christ on the cross cry out on behalf of those who crucified Him, "Father, forgive them; for they do not know what they are doing."[9]

Now Peter had the opportunity to accept Christ's forgiveness for himself. Jesus had prayed that Peter's faith would not fail. And in the aftermath of the crucifixion, this heartbroken disciple remembered the Lord's words and turned back to Him, believing that he was still loved and forgiven in spite of everything.

Peter must have also learned of the totality of Christ's love, a love that "does not take into account a wrong suffered."[10] Jesus didn't throw Peter's failure in his face. In fact, the Bible does not record Christ ever mentioning the denials after the Last Supper—a wonderful fulfillment of God's promise that He will remove our sins as far as the east is from the west and will "remember [our sins] no more."[11]

In vivid contrast, Satan loves to make the most of our failures, for through them he can fully assume his role as "the accuser of our brethren," causing us to think, *I'm totally inadequate… I'm just not "spiritual" enough… I don't know enough… I'm not doing enough for God…*

But the Lord Jesus Christ justifies and accepts us and can even use our failures for His glory. J. C. Metcalfe said:

> Without a bitter experience of our own inadequacy and
> poverty [we] are quite unfitted to bear the burden of spiritual
> ministry. It takes a man who has discovered something of the
> measures of his own weakness to be patient with the foibles of
> others.
>
> Such a man also has a first-hand knowledge of the loving
> care of the Chief Shepherd, and His ability to heal one who
> has come humbly to trust in Him and Him alone.
> Therefore he does not easily despair of others, but looks

beyond sinfulness, willfulness and stupidity, to the might of unchanging love.

The Lord Jesus does not give the charge, "Be a shepherd to My lambs…to My sheep," on hearing Peter's self-confident affirmation of undying loyalty, but He gives it after he has utterly failed to keep his vows and has wept bitterly in the streets of Jerusalem.[12]

I have often put myself in Peter's place, and I can relate closely to all that he went through—how he watched the Lord from a distance, failed Him, and wondered how God could possibly love him and use him again.

After Jean reminded me about God's love and forgiveness despite our failures, I decided to meditate on scriptures that spoke of God's perfect love for me. As I did, His love cast out any fear in my heart.[13] I came to see that God loves me as I am, just as He loved Peter as he was, and that He forgives me, just as He forgave Peter. The Lord looks beyond my failures and inconsistencies into my heart attitude of repentance and my sincere desire to please Him.

Wherever we are right now, no matter how we may feel, we are loved and forgiven. We are "right on schedule" according to God's timetable. He who has begun a good work in us will continue to perform it.[14] The Lord will not forsake the work of His own hands.

Just as Peter knew when he recognized Christ on the seashore, it is never too late to "swim" to Him.

It is never too late to begin again.

CHAPTER 10

How Firm a Foundation?

I had been invited to speak at a student conference in Washington, D.C. Following the conference, a good friend, Winky Leinster, and I decided to take a Sunday drive across the Virginia countryside. Winky started out as the driver, and after one of the stops I offered to drive.

The lovely green rolling hills, with quaint farmhouses tucked back in groves of trees, made the outing thoroughly enjoyable. As we came over a hill, we were basking in the beauty of our surroundings only to see several police cars on the grassy median of the freeway.

"Uh-oh, Wink. I think this is a speed trap. I'm going over sixty, and this is a fifty-five-miles-per-hour speed zone. I think I'm in trouble."

As we passed, one of the police cars pulled out immediately, its red light flashing.

I pulled off the road onto the shoulder. My heart was pounding.

A nice-looking, dark-haired highway patrolman approached the car—a light green Chevrolet that Winky affectionately called Sweet Pea. I rolled down my window.

The officer's manner was matter-of-fact and his face expressionless as he asked, "May I see your driver's license?"

I handed it to him through the window. He looked it over intently. "You wear contacts?"

"Yes."

He looked closely at my eyes to verify my statement. "You're from out of state?"

"Yes, I live in California. I'm just here on a brief visit."

"Did you know you were going seventy miles an hour in a fifty-five zone?"

"I know I was going over sixty, but I don't think I was going seventy."

"We clocked you at seventy miles an hour, and you'll have to come with me into the next town to see the magistrate. Since you're from out of town, you'll have to face charges today."

"The magistrate? Officer, we're on our way back to D.C., where I need to catch a plane in the morning. Can't I settle this with you? I really don't have time to spare."

"I'm sorry, but you will have to follow me into town to see the magistrate."

By this time I was groping for a way to get off the hook. "My dad's a lawyer. Isn't there some way I could take care of this with you and settle it by mail?"

Unimpressed with my parentage and unmoved by my pleas, the officer said, "No, I'm sorry. You'll have to come with me to see the magistrate."

"How long do you think this will take?"

"It depends on how long it takes us to locate her and how busy she is. Now, if you'll just follow me into town."

He started walking back to his car. I took a deep breath and restarted the engine.

"Well, he was all business, wasn't he?" Winky said supportively. "Nothing seemed to matter to him. All he was concerned about was that the law was broken and that you need to go before the judge."

As we followed the patrolman mile after mile into town, I began to feel as if I were in a bad dream.

"Wink, I can't believe this is happening."

"Neither can I."

"This is unreal, getting taken into a magistrate! I've never heard anyone use that title before. Usually they say *judge*." I ventured, "Let's pray." We proceeded to thank the Lord for our predicament, and asked Him for grace and favor in the eyes of the magistrate.

We came into the business district of Culpeper, passing hamburger stands and service stations before heading into the older part of town.

As we rounded a corner, we saw a quaint, old two-story courthouse that appeared to come out of another era. Surrounding the building was an equally old wrought-iron fence with a sign on it that loomed large: JAIL IN REAR.

The officer preceded us through the gate and headed around the building toward the back.

"Wink, do you see that? Jail! We're headed for the jail! I can't believe this."

As we disembarked from the car, we tromped over a cobblestone path and through a dilapidated door to face immediately a large, long white counter. Behind it, our arresting officer was telephoning the magistrate.

We stood in front of the counter, taking in the setting. Close by on our left were iron bars and cells. Through the opening we could hear prisoners talking.

The wall behind us was covered with—of all things—"Wanted" posters. The gray, solemn faces stared out at us, complete with numbers and statistics.

"Miss Bailey, I need to ask you some questions."

I turned toward the counter to see the officer holding some forms on a clipboard. He started asking me some questions. When he asked who my employer was, a bit embarrassed, I said, "Believe it or not, I work with Campus Crusade for Christ International."

This was the first time I had seen even a glimmer of a smile in his eyes. But he made no reply.

After I'd answered the rest of the questions, I said, "I see you have a coffee maker just like mine. Makes great coffee." My comment seemed to break the ice further and soften his businesslike manner. Warmly he offered, "Would you like a cup?"

"Yes, I'd love one. Thank you."

He gave me the coffee and continued standing at the counter facing the front door, recording something on his clipboard. His writing was interrupted when the door flew open and a large, gray-haired woman came barreling through like a cyclone. She stepped over the threshold and continued toward her inner office. Without so much as a glance in the officer's direction, she blurted out in rapid-fire succession the words, "Do-you-swear-to-tell-the-truth-the-whole-truth-and-nothing-but-the-truth-so-help-you-God?"

The officer was just responding with his customary "I do" as the woman went into her office. Winky said something about wondering if he didn't feel a little foolish with his right hand stuck up in the air while the judge was already two rooms away. It seemed as if we were living out a scene from a situation comedy. I whispered to Winky, "Try not to laugh." We succeeded—but it was difficult!

We had been waiting about ten minutes when the officer, who had remained with us, said, "You can go in now."

As we walked into the magistrate's office, she did not look up or say a word or acknowledge us in any way. I wondered if the officer hadn't sent us in prematurely. Winky and I exchanged quizzical glances. I almost felt invisible as we stood shifting from one foot to the other for ten more minutes while the judge busied herself with papers on her desk.

Then without looking up, she said authoritatively, "You were going seventy miles an hour in a fifty-five-miles-an-hour zone. That will be fifty dollars or a day in jail."

I had figured my finances while we were waiting in the lobby, and responding with some relief, I said, "Well, amazingly enough, that's just about what I have in my checking account."

She looked up abruptly as I reached for my purse and spoke with a tone of disgust. "We can't take your check!"

"You can't?" I said with astonishment. "It would be perfectly good, and I have all kinds of identification."

"That doesn't matter. We don't take out-of-state checks. You'll have to spend the night in jail!"

Winky and I looked at each other in dismay.

"I'm a Virginia resident," Winky offered. "My parents live in Vienna, Virginia. Can you take my check?"

"No. What about your parents? Could they send money?"

"I'm sure they would if they could, but they are en route to South Carolina. There is no possible way I could reach them before tomorrow."

The magistrate looked back at me and said firmly, "You'll have to spend the night in jail."

I knew I had no choice. I had broken the law. It didn't matter to the judge who I was, what my occupation was, or that my father was a lawyer. My identification and checks were unacceptable. I couldn't pay the penalty. I would have to go to jail. That was all there was to it.

I thought, *This will be a first! Wait until my friends hear about this!*

The policeman, who had entered the room a few minutes earlier, stepped forward and told Winky, "If you want to write me a personal check for fifty dollars, I'll cash it for you out of my pocket. And then you'll have the money to pay the fine."

"Why can you cash a check and she can't?" I asked the policeman, while motioning to the magistrate.

"Because I'm offering to do this personally and not as a part of the court."

Before he had a chance to change his mind, Winky took him up on his offer. She wrote out a check for fifty dollars, and he handed her fifty dollars in cash. Then Winky, in turn, gave the fifty dollars to the magistrate and paid my penalty for me. She gave us a receipt marked "Paid in full."

At last, I was free to go!

The officer walked out the door with us. His parting words were, "Ladies, from now on try not to speed."

I felt as if I had been through the wringer. When we reached our car, I smiled and said, "I've driven enough for one day. You drive."

As we pulled away from the courthouse, we prayed once again, thanking God for all we had been through. We asked Him to teach us from the experience. As we began to discuss what had just happened, we realized that what Winky had done for me illustrated what Christ had done for us on the cross.

I had broken the law by speeding and was sentenced to pay the penalty of fifty dollars or spend a day in jail. Since I couldn't pay the penalty, Winky paid it for me. All I had to do was accept what she had done for me—which I gladly did.

In like manner, we have all broken God's laws and must pay the penalty, which is death. But God sent Christ to die for our sins, to pay the penalty for us as a gift. All we need to do is accept Him and what He's done for us on the cross.

Yet many people don't understand how to become a Christian, like the woman who said to her friend, "I'm not born again yet, but I keep trying and trying!" This woman did not realize that becoming a Christian is so simple a child can understand the process. It's a matter of believing in Jesus Christ and saying yes to Him.

God often has people cross my path who are not yet Christians but who are spiritually hungry and want to know God. But the most memorable time was the night of the Big Thompson flood when I had my conversation with the woman whom Jackie Hudson had helped on that dark, slippery mountain.

I was talking with her when the police ordered us to get into our cars immediately and line up in a caravan to wait for further instructions. As I raced the fifty yards to the car, I thought that I would never see the woman again. It was very cold and raining hard, and I was relieved that the car started with ease. (It hadn't always!)

To my surprise, when I returned to the point where the caravan was forming, the woman, her husband, and Jackie Hudson got in my car to wait.

They had been in the car only a few seconds when her husband said, "I'm going to see if I can find our trailer up ahead. I've got some whiskey in there, and I need it."

As he shut the door, the woman said again, "Who are you and why are you being so good to us?"

"We are staff members with Campus Crusade for Christ, an interdenominational Christian organization," I answered. "We came here today for a retreat and were staying just across the river at the Sylvan Dale Ranch when we heard the warnings to evacuate. Some of our women are still on the other side, and we're concerned about them."

"I've heard of your group. I've been a church member for years."

"May I ask you a question? In all your years of being a church member, have you ever come to know Christ personally, for yourself?"

She shook her head. "I've been in church all my life, but I don't think I know Him like you're talking about."

"I don't know how much time we have, but let me tell you how you can know Him."

It was dark, the windows were foggy, and we could barely see each other's faces as I began. "The first thing is that God loves you. John 3:16 says, 'For God so loved the world, that He gave His only begotten Son, that whoever believes in Him should not perish, but have eternal life.' You can replace *world* with your own name. By the way"—I smiled—"what is your name?"

"Lou."

"Then the verse would read, 'For God so loved Lou, that He gave His only begotten Son, that if Lou believes in Him, she should not perish, but have eternal life.'

"It's like this, Lou." In the condensation on the windshield I drew two parallel lines, one across the top and one at the bottom. "God is up here, way above us, and He is holy. Men and women are down here, and we are sinful."

I drew some arrows from the lower portion, reaching about halfway up the windshield. "We try to reach up to God in a number of ways, but the Bible says we all have sinned and have fallen short of the glory of God.[1] Basically that means that none of us is as good as God is, and we are prone to go our own way with little or no thought of God.

"The Bible also says we earn something for our sin. 'For the wages of sin is death, but the free gift of God is eternal life in Christ Jesus our Lord.'[2]

Her eyes were glued on me as she listened intently.

I continued, "*Sin* was a word that quite frankly used to bother me. I didn't like it at all. Then someone told me to imagine putting everything I've ever done in my life on film, projecting the movie on a large screen, and inviting all my family, neighbors, and friends to come see it. Now, if you are like me, there would be some things you wouldn't want them to see!"

"Oh yes," she exclaimed. "There are things I wouldn't want to see up there."

"Well," I replied, "those are the things that the Bible calls sin. Those are the things Jesus died for." Then I superimposed the cross of Christ between the parallel lines, illustrating how Jesus had paid the penalty for our sin, our separation, bridging the gap between God and man. "When I first saw that, Lou—that Jesus bridges the gap—I finally understood where Jesus fit into the picture. It had never made sense to me before.

"Jesus is God's only provision for our sin, and through Him we can know God's love and plan for our lives. You've probably heard that He said: 'I am the way, and the truth, and the life; no one comes to the Father, but through Me.'"[3]

"Yes, I've heard that."

"It's not enough to know these things. We may have grown up hearing them. You know, many people will tell us we ought to become Christians, but very few people ever tell us *how.* And this is the last and most important point—the how-to. We must individually receive Jesus Christ as Savior and Lord by personal invitation. That means that no one else can receive Him for us.

"Jesus said, 'Behold, I stand at the door and knock.' That is the door to your heart and life. 'If anyone hears My voice and opens the door…' And we either will or we won't; it is a matter of our wills. Christ says, 'I will come in.'[4] Lou, do you think you'd like to ask Him into your life?"

"Oh yes, and I'd like to do that right now."

"We receive Christ by faith, Lou, and our faith can be expressed through prayer, which is talking to God. Why don't you pray, asking Christ to come into your life? Then Jackie and I will pray for you."

She began, "Lord Jesus, I need You. I thank You for dying for me and for all those things that would be up on the screen of my life. I ask You to come into my life, forgive my sins, and be my Savior and my Lord."

I prayed, "Lord, thank You for letting us meet Lou tonight. I thank You that You have heard her prayer and have come into her heart. Thank You for Your promise that You will never leave her nor forsake her and that You will be with her always."

Jackie, through tears of joy, continued our prayer from the backseat. "Lord, thank You that Lou has made the most important decision of her life tonight. If we never see her again, we will see her again in heaven."

When we finished praying, I asked, "Lou, where is Jesus Christ right now in relation to you?"

Smiling broadly, she said, "He's in my heart."

"That's right. And how do you know He's there?"

"Because I asked Him in, and I feel Him."

"Yes, and if the feelings were gone in the morning, you would know He is still there because He promised He would come in, and He doesn't lie. Not only did He come in, but He has promised never to leave you nor forsake you. All those things that would have been up on the screen of your life are not there anymore, because Jesus has forgiven you. You have a clean screen, a new beginning—and that's good news!"

"Yes, it is," she smiled. "This is wonderful. I'd like to get your address."

The very moment we finished exchanging addresses, her husband opened the car door and said, "Let's go. The police are getting ready to lead us out of here."

After the ten minutes that the Lord gave us together, Lou

left with the light of Christ shining in her eyes and on her countenance.

Jackie moved up to the front seat and said, "Ney, the whole atmosphere was full of love as you talked with Lou. It was as though the Lord set a moment of time aside, and just for that moment the flood wasn't here."

We marveled together over the Lord's perfect timing.

On that cold night of fear and death, in the midst of trauma, this dear woman discovered God's love for her.

The following Christmas, Lou sent me a small package containing two handmade crosses, one gold and one silver, along with a note, saying, "One is for you, and one is for Jackie. Thank you for all you did to help me the night of the flood."

After the flood Marilyn Henderson shared with me something Jesus had said, "For whoever wishes to save his life shall lose it; but whoever loses his life for My sake and the gospel's shall save it."[5] I was familiar with the verse, but because of the flood, the part about "losing my life for the gospel's sake" stood out to me.

My life had been spared three times that night: when I got out of the building before it was filled to the ceiling with water and mud, when I made it across the bridge before it was swept away, and when I heard the directions to get out of my car and up to higher ground. My life had been spared for a purpose.

My experiences the night of the flood caused me to think through in a new way Jesus Christ's command to go into all the world and preach the gospel.[6] In a new and deeper way I found myself saying, "Lord, for the rest of my life I want to give my life for the sake of the gospel. Use my life to help reach the world for You."

Since that time I've found God is fulfilling that pivotal prayer as I have opportunities to go throughout the world to share the love of Christ with others.

It is very interesting to me that Jesus concluded His Sermon on the Mount by speaking of a flood. He said,

> Therefore everyone who hears these words of Mine, and acts upon them, may be compared to a wise man, who built his house upon the rock. And the rain descended, and the floods came, and the winds blew, and burst against that house; and yet it did not fall, for it had been founded upon the rock. And everyone who hears these words of Mine, and does not act upon them, will be like a foolish man, who built his house upon the sand. And the rain descended, and the floods came, and the winds blew, and burst against that house; and it fell, and great was its fall.[7]

If we act upon God's Word, if we take Him at His word, we will be wise, and our lives will be solidly set on the rock of His words. If we don't take Him at His word—if we rely on our circumstances and feelings rather than what the Bible tells us, we will be foolish, building our lives upon the sand. It's really that simple.

Most of us will never go through a real flood, but we will all go through the "floods of life." While we are in our personal floods, God wants us to take Him at His word, believing that what He says is truer than how we feel or any circumstance we will ever face, because:

HEAVEN AND EARTH WILL PASS AWAY,
BUT HIS WORD WILL NOT PASS AWAY.[8]

TWELVE-WEEK
BIBLE STUDY

LESSON 1

Read chapter 1, "The Flood," in *Faith Is Not a Feeling* at least once.

1. In this chapter Ney describes a time of tragedy in her life. Write a brief account of an emotional or physical tragedy in your own life.

2. When the flood swept through Ney's life, she made the choice not to live by her feelings but to take God at His word. The following three verses encouraged Ney to make this choice. Meditate on each verse, and personalize each one in the form of a prayer to God. The first verse is done for you.

   a. 1 Thessalonians 5:18: "In everything give thanks; for this is God's will for you in Christ Jesus."

   God, You ask me to make a choice by my will to thank You, even when I don't feel like it. This is really hard for me to do, but I want to learn to thank You and accept Your will for me. I know this will bring peace to my life.

   b. Romans 8:28

   c. Matthew 24:35

3. What difference would it have made in your tragic situation if you had applied the three verses you wrote about in question two?

4. Hebrews 13:15 encourages you to offer a sacrifice of thanksgiving.

   a. Look up the word *sacrifice* in the dictionary, and write a definition here.

   b. Think about a problem you are facing now. Explain how you could offer a sacrifice of thanksgiving to God in the midst of your problem.

5. What did you learn from this chapter about believing that God's Word is truer than how you feel? Do you think this can make a difference in how you deal with problems in your life? Explain how.

LESSON 2

Read chapter 2, "Arizona Agony."

1. Memorize Ephesians 5:18.

2. Describe a time when you felt like giving up.

3. Ney thought, "If only I can change my circumstances, things will get better." List three "if onlys" in your life now.

a. If only

b. If only

c. If only

4. Failure often points us to the truth that we cannot live the Christian life on our own. What do the following verses teach you about this truth?

a. John 14:16-18

b. John 14:26

c. 2 Timothy 1:7

   d. 2 Corinthians 12:9-10

5. How could understanding and applying the verses listed under question four keep you from feeling defeated and falling into an "if only" mentality?

6. Write your memory verse (Ephesians 5:18) here. What does it mean to you to be filled with the Spirit?

7. What has God taught you this week about failure?

LESSON 3

Read chapter 3, "Just Say the Word."

1. Hebrews 11 is known as "Faith's Hall of Fame." Read all of Hebrews 11 twice. Select three people who are noted for their faith, and explain how they "took God at His word."

2. Think of a person you know who lives "by faith." List three character qualities you see in him or her.

3. Read Mark 4:35-41 twice.

   a. Why did the disciples become fearful?

   b. Describe a time in your life when you reacted like the disciples.

4. Ney makes four very important statements about faith. Choose two of these and explain what they mean to you personally.
   - God's Word is truer than anything I feel.
   - God's Word is truer than anything I experience.
   - God's Word is truer than any circumstances I will ever face.
   - God's Word is truer than anything in the world.

5. Read Mark 14:32-36. Jesus honestly expressed His feelings to the Father and then made a choice to trust God in the midst of His feelings. Think about what God has allowed in your life, and complete the following statement:

   Lord,

   I feel _____

   _____

   but Lord, Your Word says _____

   _____

   _____ .

6. Write a prayer to God expressing your desire to develop the habit of taking Him at His word.

LESSON 4

Read chapter 4, "Matters of Conscience."

1. Look up the word *conscience* in the dictionary and write the meaning here.

2. Write down ten words that describe how you feel when you have a clear conscience.

3. Read Acts 24:16. Write a paragraph describing how you could keep a blameless conscience before both God and men.

4. Write Psalm 139:23-24 here. Also write these two verses on a piece of paper you can carry with you this week. Read these verses many times, memorize them, and pray them back to God. Ask God to search your heart and see if there is anything in your life that is keeping you from having a clear conscience.

5. Ney said not to be too introspective in examining your conscience. She explained that if something needs to be made right in your relationship with God or man, it will surface effortlessly in your mind. As you read this chapter, did God bring incidents to your mind as He did to Ney?

a. If so, what were the incidents?

b. Do you think God is asking you to make things right in these situations?

c. There may be times when it is not possible or appropriate to go back to a person or to a situation as Ney did. But it is always possible to go to the Lord Himself. As Ney said, He has given us the "Christian's bar of soap" in 1 John 1:9: "If we *confess* our sins, He is faithful and righteous to *forgive* us our sins and to *cleanse* us from *all* unrighteousness" (author's emphasis).

Confess means to agree with God that He is right and you are wrong.

Forgiven and cleansed… He not only forgives us, but He cleanses us from *all* unrighteousness. What a powerful promise.

Pray and ask the Lord to search your heart and bring to mind any things in your life that are hindering your relationship with Him. Write those things on a piece of paper. Then confess them to Him, one by one. When you have finished confessing, write 1 John 1:9 across your paper, claiming His forgiveness and cleansing.

LESSON 5

Read chapter 5, "A Change of Heart."

1. Ney says that because she doubted that her father loved her, she grew to hate and resent him. Look up the word *bitterness* in the dictionary, and write a definition here.

2. Describe your own relationship with your parents.

3. Ney said, "God had chosen my parents for me! He was not surprised that I was born into my particular family. When I realized this truth, I thanked God for my parents—for the first time in my life." How do you respond to the truth that God sovereignly placed you in your particular family?

4. Write a letter to your parents, thanking God for them and also acknowledging all the things they did right. (You can go through this exercise even if your parents have passed away.)

5. Ney took the beautiful passage about love, 1 Corinthians 13:1-8, and wrote, "God's love toward me is patient." Go through 1 Corinthians 13 as Ney did but using *your name*. Check page 51 in the book to see just how Ney did this. An example follows:

God's love toward _____ (put in your name) is kind.

6. Do the same exercise with 1 Corinthians 13:1-8, but this time put in the name of a person (a parent or someone else) who has wounded you.

7. Ney said, "Though my father never asked me to forgive him of anything, the Lord asked that of me." Is God asking you to forgive the person who wounded you? Are you willing? If so, write a prayer here to express your desire to God.

LESSON 6

This week's Bible study will be different from the preceding five lessons; it is set aside as a time of *Remembrance* and *Reflection*. Throughout the Scriptures we are exhorted to remember the deeds of God, not to forget what He has taught us and what He has done for us.

1. Look back over the first five lessons, and write a paragraph as a reminder of the main truth God taught you each week.

   a. Week One

   b. Week Two

   c. Week Three

   d. Week Four

e. Week Five

2. What Scripture verses were the most meaningful to you in these lessons? Write them out here.

3. You have *Remembered*. Now it is time to *Reflect* on how these truths have affected your life. Do you see changes in your life? Write an example of a new attitude or action brought about by new truth about God and His ways.

4. Write a prayer thanking God for His work in your life.

LESSON 7

Read chapter 6, "A Brick at a Time."

1. Ney talks about vain imagination balloons, those negative thoughts that we imagine to be true and then balloon in our minds. Describe a time when you did this wrong thinking, and describe the outcome.

2. God instructs us to have right thinking. Read Philippians 4:8.

   a. Write a personal paraphrase of this verse.

   b. What difference would it have made in the situation you described under number one if you had applied the truths of Philippians 4:8?

3. What did God teach you from the story of the man who gave one-hundred-dollar bills away? (See pages 71-2.)

a. Read Romans 11:33-36. Who does it say is the Giver of all gifts?

b. What difference would it have made to the people receiving the hundred-dollar bills if they had known the truth of Romans 11:36?

4. Think of a difficult relationship in your life. Write a paragraph explaining why it is difficult for you.

5. a. Memorize Romans 15:7. Write it here.

   b. List five ways that living out Romans 15:7 would make a difference in your problem relationship.

6. Read 1 Peter 3:8-9. How can you "sow good seed" in your problem relationship? What blessing can you return for an insult? Think of two ways, and list them here.

7. Write a prayer to God expressing what you desire to learn in relating to others.

LESSON 8

Read chapter 7, "Unmasking the Enemy."

C. S. Lewis said that if Satan can get us to disbelieve his existence, he has won a major battle, because his activity goes unrecognized.

1. Read 1 Peter 5:6-10.

   a. What do you learn about Satan in this passage?

   b. What are you instructed to do in this passage?

   c. How can you resist the Enemy and stand firm in your faith?

2. This week memorize 1 Peter 5:8-9, which follows. After you memorize these verses, pray them back to God, asking Him to teach you the truth about your adversary and to show you how to resist him and to stand firm in your faith.

> Be of sober spirit, be on the alert. Your adversary, the devil, prowls about like a roaring lion, seeking someone to devour. But resist him, firm in your faith.

3. Satan sends "fiery darts" at each believer. Ney lists five of these "darts." Pick two from the following list and describe a situation in your life when the Enemy threw that particular "dart" at you. Also describe your response.

a. Doubt

b. Feeling forsaken by God

c. Having a sense of worthlessness

d. Being criticized

e. The "if only" syndrome

4. Read Ephesians 6:10-16.

a. Write a paraphrase of this passage.

b. In practical terms, how can you put on the armor of God and stand firm against the schemes of the devil? List at least three ways.

LESSON 9

Read chapter 8, "Objectifying Life's Pain."

1. This week memorize Romans 8:28.

2. If 75 percent of your life is characterized by struggles, concerns, frustrations, and trials, how can you "walk by faith" during these difficult times? List five ways.

3. Ney describes the "when-then" syndrome: "When I get out of this hard spot, *then* everything will be fine."

   a. Describe a time when you got caught up in the "when-then" syndrome.

b. What were the results?

4. Think of a problem you are facing in your life. It can be a person, a situation, or a circumstance. Read the instructions on pages 100-1 for completing the chart on page 162.

a. Find a quiet place, and ask God to guide you as you fill in the chart.

b. Fill in the chart.

c. Write out Romans 8:28 across the bottom of the chart, and thank God that this verse is His truth.

d. Spend time this week praying through *and meditating on* the scripture(s) you wrote in section four on the chart. Ask God to teach you the truth of His Word in the midst of your problem.

5. Read Matthew 6:34. Rewrite this verse in your own words as a prayer to God. (Refer to how Ney prayed this verse on pages 110-1.)

1. THINGS I LIKE	2. THINGS I DON'T LIKE
3. MY REACTIONS OR MY RESPONSES	**4.** WHAT GOD MIGHT WANT TO TEACH ME, OR SCRIPTURES TO MEET MY NEED

LESSON 10

Read chapter 9, "Failure and the Phantom."

1. This week memorize 1 John 1:9.

2. Forgiveness means "to cancel a debt as if it never happened." Read Psalm 103:10-14.

   a. Rewrite these verses in your own words, inserting your name or a reference to yourself. Verse 11 is done for you:

   "Because I reverence and fear God, His unfailing love for me is as great as the height of the heavens above the earth."

   b. Reread your paraphrase of Psalm 103:10-14. What feelings do these words produce in your heart?

3. Imagine that you are the apostle Peter.

   a. Read Luke 22:31-34 and 22:54-62. You are the apostle who failed. Describe how you are feeling about yourself.

   b. Now read Mark 16:6-7. How does the Lord's special concern for you (Peter) make you feel?

   c. Read John 21:1-7. Describe your (Peter's) reaction in John 21:7.

4. Even though Peter failed, he knew that Jesus loved and forgave him. He was so excited to see Jesus that he jumped into the sea! How can you, in spite of your failings, reach out and accept the Lord's love and forgiveness for you?

5. Write your memory verse (1 John 1:9) here. How can this verse encourage you when you fail?

LESSON 11

Read chapter 10, "How Firm a Foundation?"

1. Memorize John 3:16 this week.

a. Write John 3:16 here, inserting your name in place of the word *world*.

   b. Think of five descriptive words that express how seeing your name in John 3:16 makes you feel.

      Example: Accepted

2. On a separate piece of paper, write about the time when you received Jesus Christ as your personal Savior from sin. You might want to think about dividing the paper into three sections.

   a. What my life was like before I became a Christian

   b. How I became a Christian

   c. What my life is like since I became a Christian

3. If you have not accepted Christ's payment for your sin, reread the chapter and consider praying and inviting Christ into your life right now. If you prayed to receive Christ as your Savior today, write the date here as a record of the most important decision you will ever make.

4. Go before God in prayer, and ask Him to show you the names of those with whom you could share the Good News of salvation. Write their names here.

a. Covenant to pray for these people daily.

b. Ask God to give you an opportunity to tell another person how you came to know Christ and how your life has changed because of your relationship with Him.

LESSON 12

This week's Bible study will be different than the preceding five lessons. Like lesson six, this week is set aside as a time of *Remembrance* and *Reflection.* Throughout the Scriptures we are exhorted to remember the deeds of God, not to forget what He has taught us and what He has done for us.

1. Look back over lessons 7 through 11, and write a paragraph to remember the main truth God taught you each week.

   a. Week Seven

   b. Week Eight

c. Week Nine

d. Week Ten

e. Week Eleven

2. Which Scripture verses were the most meaningful to you in these lessons? Write them here.

3. You have *Remembered*. Now it is time to *Reflect* on how these truths have affected your life. Do you see changes in your life? Write an example of a new attitude or action brought about by new truth about God and His ways.

4. Write a prayer thanking God for His work in your life.

NOTES

CHAPTER 1: THE FLOOD

1. Now Ryderg
2. 1 Thessalonians 5:18, KJV
3. Romans 8:28
4. Matthew 24:35
5. Based on Hebrews 13:15, KJV

CHAPTER 2: ARIZONA AGONY

1. Hebrews 13:5
2. Matthew 28:20
3. Genesis 28:16

CHAPTER 3: JUST SAY THE WORD

1. Romans 1:17, KJV
2. 1 John 5:4
3. Luke 7:7
4. Luke 7:9
5. Hebrews 11:7
6. Hebrews 11:8
7. Hebrews 11:11
8. Mark 4:40

9. Matthew 24:35
10. 1 Peter 1:25
11. Isaiah 40:8
12. Jeremiah 31:3
13. 1 Corinthians 13
14. Acts 10:34
15. Matthew 26:37-38; Mark 14:33; Luke 22:44
16. Romans 8:28-29

CHAPTER 4: MATTERS OF CONSCIENCE

1. Acts 24:16
2. 1 Timothy 1:18-19
3. Proverbs 21:5-6, TLB
4. 1 John 5:14-15

CHAPTER 5: A CHANGE OF HEART

1. 1 John 4:16
2. Psalm 47:4
3. Psalm 139:13
4. Ephesians 3:14-15
5. Ephesians 6:2-3
6. Proverbs 1:8-9, NIV

CHAPTER 6: A BRICK AT A TIME

1. 1 John 1:7
2. John 10:10

3. Luke 18:1, KJV
4. 1 Thessalonians 5:18, KJV
5. Romans 8:28
6. 1 John 1:5
7. Romans 8:29
8. 1 Peter 3:8-9
9. Galatians 5:22-23
10. Psalm 133:1, KJV

CHAPTER 7: UNMASKING THE ENEMY

1. 1 John 4:4
2. This book is now out-of-print, but copies may be available through used bookstores and Web sites such as Amazon.com.
3. Matthew 6:9-14
4. John 17:15
5. Ephesians 6:10-16
6. John 8:44
7. Genesis 3:1
8. Revelation 12:10
9. Romans 8:1,31-34, author's emphasis
10. Romans 8:35-39
11. Hebrews 13:5
12. Isaiah 43:4
13. Oswald Chambers, *My Utmost for His Highest* (1935; reprint, Uhrichsville, Ohio: Barbour, 1963), 124, 328.
14. Genesis 3:1-5
15. Genesis 50:20, NIV

16. John 11:20-21,30-32
17. John 11:40, author's emphasis
18. 2 Timothy 2:25-26
19. Matthew 17:20
20. Hebrews 13:5
21. Ephesians 1:18-23

CHAPTER 8: OBJECTIFYING LIFE'S PAIN

1. John 16:33
2. Galatians 5:22-23
3. Romans 8:1
4. Brother Lawrence, *The Practice of the Presence of God* (Old Tappan, N.J.: Revell, 1958), 16.
5. Matthew 6:25,28-30
6. Matthew 6:31-33
7. Ephesians 3:20
8. Matthew 6:34

CHAPTER 9: FAILURE AND THE PHANTOM

1. 1 Corinthians 3:6-7; Ephesians 4:16
2. Romans 5:1
3. Romans 5:6-10
4. John 15:9
5. Luke 22:31-34; Matthew 26:35
6. Luke 22:54-62, author's emphasis
7. Mark 16:6-7, author's emphasis
8. John 21:1-8